ANAGRAMACRON

Weird anagrams collected by TS Caladan

2017, TWB Press
www.twbpress.com

Dedicated to listening, learning and changing when true Voices of the Universe Speak ~

Anagramacron
Copyright © 2017 by TS Caladan

This is a work of fiction. Names, characters, places, and incidences are either a product of the author's imagination or are used fictitiously. Any resemblance to any actual person, living or dead, events, or locales is entirely coincidental.

Cover Art by TS Caladan

ISBN: 978-1-944045-34-0

Contents of the Anagramacron

ANAGRAMACRON

What insights does the magic of anagrams uncover for various familiar names? What's in a name? Could be *everything.* The ancients believed anagrams revealed one's destiny or fate. Are anagrams similar to horoscopes, crystal balls, tarot cards, palmistry or Ouija boards? You decide, but only after you've seen the strange poetry.

In the age of computers, generators such as '**Anagram Genius**' have answered many mysteries. At the push of a button, every possibility is anagrammatically listed from 100% total sensibility down to 0%. Perfect or near-perfect [using each letter] anagrams should express nonsense. Phrases should be gibberish such as, "Hand me the piano, Chester" or "Make mine a flamingo" that have no connection to the person or thing anagrammed. Anagrams should be abstract 'apples' and 'oranges' that have no relationship with the subject. Instead of Dr. Seuss-type nonsensical-phrases…

Would you believe there is a direct link between perfect anagrams and the subject that is anagrammed? The "**Anagramacron**" collection will surely convince the biggest skeptic. Common sense tells us: "It's only rearranged letters!" No. It's much more. There is nothing common about the VOICE or whatever the hell is speaking to us through anagrams. But something definitely is and the results tabulated by computer-generators are fascinating. Maybe we should listen?

Examine anagrams of infamous villains. Are they negative? Why are certain anagrams of respected celebrities, leaders and heroes also very negative? Maybe anagrams aren't evil? Maybe they're pure TRUTH? Could the light of anagrams shine upon deeply buried secrets? What 'skeletons' are suddenly revealed inside hidden closets by an extraordinary method, something beyond our understanding?

Abner Doubleday = bleed a boundary…ably bonded area…bore a lane, buddy

Abraham Lincoln = ham in local barn…I'll ban a monarch…cabin hall manor…an local Brahmin…a bill anchorman

Abraham Lincoln, President = races in thralldom? I pen ban…enact on sharp, liberal mind…this American-born led plan…non-small chap, tinier beard…end Americans' ill born path…a tall diner, can be no shrimp…small, taperin' beard on chin…charitable splendor in man…partisan bill charmed none…spin brothel American land…Lord romps bicentennial…Hill banned American sport…bad historical men planner…brash manner, political end?

A Business Man = insane, bum, ass

A Confirmed Bachelor = I face no bold charmer

The Confirmed Bachelor = laced bitch? her for me? no…catch bold her? no, I'm free…female? chronic bother

Actors = co-star…sor act…or acts…trac so

Adam and Eve = even a ma, dad…evaded a man…made Nevada…evade a damn?

Adam and Eve in the Garden = man, red-handed negative

Adam Levine = a mean devil

Admiral Nelson = mean slain Lord…all Marines nod…land, sailor man…loser mainland…seaman on drill

Admiral Poindexter = I'm an expert, odd liar…Marxian, odd reptile…I'm X-rated, ideal porn…mail android expert

Adolph Hitler = rapid, hot hell…hi, lethal drop…hell had to rip…hated phor ill

Adolf Hitler = rill of death…death for ill…heil, fat lord…a droll thief...filled Torah...triad of Hell...Dr. Loath-Life...filthy ordeal...rid of, lethal...a dirt of Hell...thrilled oaf...drill of hate...do real filth...or lead filth...hated for ill...I, dart of Hell...heil, old fart...hatred of ill...I'll do father...ill doth fear

Adolf Hitler, the Austrian = filth or deadlier fatalist...Red Stalin: oh, that failure...hint: hateful, oral tirades...all hushed, fear attrition...ah, found treaties a thrill

Adolf Hitler, the German Dictator = detailed hatred forthcoming later...threat: mad art, thrill of genocide...tell Dott, a manager of Third Reich

A. Hitler = the liar...heil, rat!

Adolph Hitler Schicklgruber = group's Third Reich black Hell

Hitler and the Nazis = enthrall in this daze

Agatha Christie = rich hag is at tea...is a theatric hag...ah, hate is tragic

A Giant's Leftfielder = I felt a federal sting

A Homeless Person = hopeless moaners...lonesome phrases...or hopeless means...or lameness hopes...O, no ser, me hapless

A Knight in Shining Armour = human in iron. risk hit, gang

Alanis Morissette = is a solemn artiste...Miss Sole Attainer...one aimless artist...a starlet emission...no aimless artiste...it's nasal, tiresome...a real mess to sit in...as into master lies...listens to same air...am staler, noisiest...lame artist noises...noisiest, lame star...I'm a tastiness role...let's, I'm a noise star...more Satanist lies...Miss Tolerate-A-Sin...retaliations mess...ta, I'm artless noise...arse, tits, semolina...SOS, I'm a senile tart

Albert Camus = am scrutable...ma scru table

Albert Einstein = ten elite brains...Elite Brains.net...N.B. Israeli tenet...stern alien, I bet

Albert A. Einstein = sentential libera...neat, elite brains...elite, insane brat...internal beastie...is an alien better?

Albert Abraham Einstein = brainiest, able Earthman...a brain in the able master...I am near the ablest brain...the real, main beast-brain

Einstein = I intense

Albert Einstein, the Physicist = it is he, the best saintly prince...I bet he's the sly ancient spirit...the sensible Anti-Christ piety...the shiniest, pantheistic celebrity...shh, brain type; elite scientist...then shiniest respectability...shiniest celebrity in the past...he is the Beast, isn't it princely?

Alec Guinness = genuine class...genius lances...genius cleans

Aleister Crowley = correlate wisely...wrote really ices...yell, wise creator...erotically sewer...well, rare society...rosy, erectile law...erotic years well...wire select Royal...wiser, loyal, erect...I recreates lowly...we Yetis Caroller

Aleister Crowley (Edward Alexander Crowley) and the Abbey of Thelema = the demon Abracadabra, lean of eye: red-hot, wet sex, lewdly crawl eerily

Alexander Graham Bell = real bad hex, all rang me

Alexander Hague = aha, deluxe anger

Alexander the Great = extra-hated general...axed the rare temple

Alexandre Dumas = a sex 'n duel drama...asexual, mad nerd

Alfred Tennyson = flay sonnet nerd

Al Gore = glee to a brr...brr to eagle...re: global rat...get laborer

Al Gore, Senator = treason galore...a great loser, no?

Al Gore, Vice President = eviler, second-rate pig...second-rate privilege

Al and Tipper Gore = preparing to lead

Alfred Nobel = label of nerd

Al Green = general

Alice Cooper = I, a cool creep

Alicia Keys = I cak easily…i.e. a sick lay…lay a sickie…I, a silky ace

Alicia Silverstone = erotica villainess…lass in evil erotica…action serial evils…is evil, erotic nasal…vitals are silicone…silica revelations…all I covet is a siren…as realistic in love

Alison Moyet = is a lot money…Oo, I'm Stanley…it's me, a loony…one moist lay…noisy to male…yes, I'm on a lot…lay emotions…solo, anytime…I, my neat solo…in meaty solo

Al Pacino = I, anal cop…a pal, icon…coin a pal

Al Yankovic = yak in vocal

Weird Al Yankovic = clownery via a kid…deviancy or I walk…direly vain wacko…wide lack in ovary…a virile, wonky cad

Amelie Mauresmo = use a male, I'm more…arouse me, I'm male

Amelie Mauresmo, World-Ranked Tennis Player = reputedly a real woman? more like a man in dress

Americans = are manics

America's Cartoonists = no artists are as comic

Amerigo Vespucci = cove is pure magic…I'm veg as occupier

Amish = I sham

Amy Semple McPherson = nymph replaces memos…me corpse's lame nymph…me cheeps manly romp…compels as mere nymph…men mess, cheaply romp…hymens compel a sperm…me charm sloppy semen… me leprose scam nymph

An American = man in a race…earn, maniac

An Astrophysicist = topic's a shiny star…any star's his topic…Oh, I spy star antics

Astrophysicist = Oh, it's spicy star…O, this spicy star…it is star psycho

Anders Celsius = rued scaliness…runs scales, dies…scale's under SI…scales in use, Dr.

Andre Agassi = grass: an aide…darn, is a sage…as age drains…is as a danger…as an aged Sir

Andy Roddick = dinky odd arc

Andy Warhol = oh, drawn lay…ha, draw only…a holy drawn…a randy howl…had only war…raw and holy…ha, yawn Lord

Angelina Jolie = I join anal glee

Anglican Ministers = malign certain sins

An Insurance Agent = entrancing nausea

Anne Rice = re: canine

Ann Landers = slander Ann

Ann Margaret = an arrant gem

Antagonist = not against…stagnation

Anthony Kiedis = he is tiny and OK…I, hedonistic yank…is a thin donkey

Anthony Hopkins = skin hat on? phony

Sir Anthony Hopkins = his tiny pranks, Oh no

Antonio Banderas = no brains on a date

Antonio Lucio Vivaldi = violin, viola aid count…ciao, vaunt violin idol

Antonio Vivaldi, Italian Composer = I'm a poetic star on violin and viola…artistic poem on a violin and viola

An Unmarried Man = I am a damn runner

An Unmarried Woman = a un-won man-admirer

A Psychiatrist = sit, chat, pay, sir…it is hasty crap

Ara Parseghian = a piranhas' rage

Archbishop of Canterbury = preach choirboy brats fun…Abbot of prayers in church…son of cherub by patriarch

A Religious Fundamentalist = I'm a futile anus, *God isn't real*

Ariel Sharon = oh, ran Israel…share no liar…rash, earn oil…shorn aerial…Iran has role…real hairs? no…ah, Iran loser

Ariel Sharon, the Prime Minister of Israel = Palestinian terrorism! fire him, arsehole!

Ariel Scheinerman = I'm Israel enhancer…I am a lecher, sinner

Army Reserve = merry as ever

Arnold Palmer = man rolled par…all modern par

Arnold Daniel Palmer = earn damn dollar pile…darn me, I'd no parallel

Arnold Schwarzenegger = he's grown large 'n crazed…grr, he's now crazed angel…crazed leghorns gnawer…Wagner scherzo dangler…screen hazard grew long

Arthur Ashe = a heart rush

Arthur Dent = hard nutter…truth 'n dare…a truth nerd

Arthur Matthews = warm as the truth…ha, warmest truth…ah, truest warmth

Arturo Toscanini = no curio, an artist…oration, curtains…narration coitus

A Shoplifter = has to pilfer

Ashton Kutcher = recast hot hunk

A Strip-Teaser = sparse attire…a prettier ass

Astronaut = unto a star…U.N. to a star…a rat, to sun

Astronomer = Moon starer

Astronomers = morons stare…a moron rests…no more stars…on more stars…Moon starers…Moon arrests…re: Moon, stars…more stars, no?

A Supermodel = O, pure damsel

A Telephone Girl = repeating 'hello'

Atilla the Hun = I, lethal haunt

Auric Goldfinger = gold ring, a 'ucifer…a gold 'ucifer ring

Axl Rose = oral sex…so relax

Ayatollah Khomeini = ak, I hate holy oilman…hail, hail, to a monkey

Babe Ruth = he rub bat…bah, brute

Bad Girls = I grab LSD

Barack Obama = aback Rambo…bomb rack, aaa…aka bomb in car…O, am back Arab

Barack Hussein Obama = a nice Arab's ambush, OK…abuse

main Arab, shock…abuse sick Arab, O man…nob abuser, a CIA sham…bash CIA base, ran amok…a braincase Bush, amok…Arabs back in USA home…so America, a Bush bank…I'm a bush snake, a cobra…maniac BHO breaks USA…maniacs broke USA, bah…a bum raise bank chaos…karma ebb, chaos in USA…bask, a no-Bush America…banker's IOU scam, ba, ha…O, I mash bareback anus…so sack a humane rabbi…babushkas on America…B.O., USA-Caesar, bank him…a man hacks our babies…nice Arab, amok as Bush…Arab Osama Bin, he suck…ambush as nice Arab, OK…Abraham is back: one USA…O, I back sub-Saharan me…O, Cuba ranks him as Abe…Bush: I can break Osama…I am a hack, abuser, snob…ban America's Bush, A-OK… I'm an Arab SOB…has Samurai backbone…O, Arab snake, ambush…I Arab sham, beckon USA…a Bohemian Arab sucks

Barack Obama, President = bad skeptic or mean Arab…O, I embrace mad Pakistan…an Arab-backed imposter…pick best man, adore Arab

Barack Hussein Obama, President = Iran adapts each bomb, nuke rises…macabre banks or USA in deep shit…ban Arab's mocker, us in deep shit…he bankrupted Americans, is a SOB…this ebon sucker made Arabs pain…breakpoint, USA became in shards…abused American banks to perish…N. Korea base, disturbance, mishap…a practice heads Iran's nuke bomb…America had ebb, stop's Iran nuke…Shaman probates banker suicide…he's boss in bankrupted America…a Democrat speaks inane rubbish…Nubian's dark hope bests America…one can repair bad Bush mistakes?…brain asks: American hope busted?

Barbara Schett, Tennis Player = pretty snatch. rather be a lesbian

Barbra Streisand = bad star is barren…bar-strained bars…a rabbi's star nerd…Babs, randier star…drab, aberrant sis…transbarbarised

Bartender = render tab

Bartenders = beer 'n darts

Bartholomeu Dias = Oh, made out Brasil

Bart Simpson = brat, imp's son...star, imp, snob

Basil Rathbone = oh, ablest brain...halo best brain...hot, able brains...this banal bore

Batman and Robin = not bad, brain man

Beatles = able set...be stale?

John, Paul, George and Ringo = golden ganja, heroin group

The Beatles: Paul McCartney, George Harrison, Ringo Starr and the late John Lennon = re-arranges nicely, shall let them be a darn great group, then? no one on chart?

McCartney, Lennon, Harrison and Starr = northern land manners 'n aristocracy...darn neat, carnal, synchrotron men, sir...manly, satanic Northerners, darn corn...northern raciness can randomly rant...so dynamic 'n carnal northern ranters

Beatles on Ed Sullivan = undatable loveliness

Beer Vendors = revere Bonds

Bela Lugosi = I'll abuse, go...I'll use a bog...a glib louse

Belinda Carlisle = ideal brain cells...incredible as all...brilliance deals...led as brilliance...alas, nice, ill-bred

Ben Stiller, the Actor = rich talent, best role

Betty and Barney Hill = ya, hell-bent banditry...hell, by neat banditry...ya, hell-bent, tiny drab...held by brainy talent

Betty Boop = pretty boob

Betty Grable = leg, Battery B...leg be by tart...by leg-art bet

Beyonce Knowles = coy, blew on knees

Beyonce Gisele Knowles = obscene eye, swelling OK…

Beyonce Knowles, the Singer = we like songs, encore by then

Big Brother and the Holding Company Featuring Janis Joplin = high in public, for they're prone to big ganja joint and LSD, man

Bill Gates = legal bits…glib Tesla…gets a bill

Billy Idol = I bold lily

Billy Ocean = lilac ebony

Billy the Kid = killed by hit

Bing Crosby = sobbing cry…song by crib

Bob Dylan = bald, bony…nobly bad…bland boy…knobby lad

Bob Marley = bomb early

Bonnie and Clyde = blonde n' cyanide…bad n' nicely done

Bonnie Parker = broken in rape

Bono = O, nob…boon…noob…no B.O.

Bono, David 'the Edge' Evans, Adam Clayton and Larry Mullen Junior = aha, just a legendary very cool Ireland band (on MTV) in a muddle, no?

Boris Badenov = absorbed vino

Boris Becker, the Tennis Player = star penis, celebrity knob, here…therein spin by racketeer lobs

Boris Yeltsin = riot sensibly

Boris Yeltsin, President = endless, insobriety trip…tipsiness done terribly…tiny beer, tipsiness lord…terribly pissed tension…one isn't terribly pissed?

Boris Nicolayevich Yeltsin = heavy insobriety kills icon

Boris Nicolayevich Yeltsin, President = thirty icy vodkas: lay prone, insensible

Botha = Oh, bat

Boy and Girl = godly brain...boy darling...a blind orgy...groin badly...gay or blind...a girly bond

Boyfriend = finer body

Boy George and Culture Club = a once-cute, burly, old bugger

Boys and Girls = boys, darlings

Brain Surgeon = boring a nurse...I grab neurons...bruise 'n organ

Brett Favre = free TV brat

Brian Eno = one brain

Brian Wilson = slow in brain...low in brains...Blair's in now...now in Brasil?

British Au Pair = I rip a USA birth

Britney Spears = best PR in years...nip yer breasts...teeny bra rips...pert, yes brains...betray in press

Bruce Lee = rue celeb...cue rebel

Bruce Springsteen = bursting presence!

Bruce Wayne, Batman = became a brawny nut

Bruce Willis = I screw, I bull

Buffy, the Vampire Slayer = pithy female braves fury

Burt Lancaster = blunt rare acts...blunt star race...act turns abler...reluctant bars

Burt Reynolds = sturdy, nobler…blunt, sore, dry…nob's truly red…rend robustly

Burt Ward = braw turd

Buster Douglas = absolute drugs…so blasted guru

James Buster Douglas = judges, amateur slobs…O Jesus, sad, brutal gem…judges' rules, am boast

Buster Keaton = but no retakes…broken statue…break out nets…best nature, OK?

Butch Cassidy and the Sundance Kid = dud, dusty technicians chased bank…deducted U.S. city banks, cash in hand…dudes snatch city cash, bunk and die

Cal Ripken = Prince Kal

Cameron Diaz = crazed, I moan…I am crazed, no?

Camilla and Charles = anarchical, mad sell

Camilla Parker Bowles = I'm Palace balls worker…came like pro, raw balls…Balmoral screw like pa…we, Balmoral parks lice…Balmoral prick weasel…swipe a Balmoral clerk…we lack real aplomb, sir…wreck pair, so all blame

Candy Samples = my landscapes

Captain James Cook = I am ocean's top Jack…joke: I, a map, can cost…point a jam sea-cock…join me, pack. a coast!

Captain James T. Kirk = maniac parks jet kit

Captain John Smith and Pocahontas = champs join hands to patch a nation

Captains of Industry = typo frauds sit in can

Carl Lewis = swill race…wills race…will: races

ANAGRAMACRON

Carlos Santana = carnal sonatas…Satan rascal, no?

Carpenter = rap centre

Catherine of Aragon = a nag to force an heir…a foreign anachoret…I fear a throne can go…another force again

Cat Stevens = events cast

Cat Stevens, Yusuf Islam = says music events: fault

Charlemagne = ache mangler…he, calm anger…me archangel…change realm…helm carnage

Charles Dickens = he's slick dancer…cheer kind class…check lardiness…darkens clichés…kids clench ears

Charles Dickens, Author = he inks loud characters…rash centuries-old hack…hear old Chaucer stinks…such dark 'n heroic tales…in a cruel hatred, shocks…thick, rude rascal shone…rather slick nude chaos…oh, characters dine, sulk…elder hack's urchin, 'Oats?'

Charles Dodgson = scholar Godsend…codger Don lashs…charges old dons…ogled dons' char?

Charles Lutwidge Dodgson = *as gold, seducing the world*…dud gent weds a schoolgirl…now chastise drugged doll…college don sad with drugs…select odd words, laughing…old dog watches nude girls…he wants 'good girl' cuddles…gets dud, so Caroll whinged…was dud college's don right?

The Reverend Charles Dodgson, Lewis Carroll = Oh, he's clever: records Wonderland girl's tale

The Reverend Dodgson aka Lewis Carroll = looks at girl, verses reached Wonderland

English Author and mathematician Charles Lutwidge Dodgson = has got on him the magical drugs that Alice used in Wonderland

Author Charles Lutwidge Dodgson, Lewis Carroll = a girl called Alice sets through wondrous world

Charles Manson = or, men can slash…harm clean sons…slash n' romance…conman hassle

Charlie Sheen = hence he's liar

Charlton Heston = on the NRA's cloth…letch sat on horn

Cheerleaders = here declares…cheers dealer…sheer declare…'e lecher's dear

Chelsea Clinton = accent is on Hell…seen all, not chic…cleanin' clothes…*clone* isn't a lech?

Chiang Kai-Shek = aha, sick King, eh?

Chief Inspector = infer cop ethics…Prince of Ethics…cop's finer ethic…pest of nice rich

Child Star = Christ lad…child's art…rich lad, ST

Chris Evert = server itch…her TV cries

Chris Martin = I, rich 'n smart…smart in rich

Chris Martin, the Coldplay Singer = last CD? crap! I ignore lines, rhythm

Chris Martin and Gwyneth Paltrow = O man, wry star pregnant with child…starry woman pregnant with child…want a child? try his worm: pregnant!

Chris Martin and Gwyneth Paltrow Become Parents = contact grim star, why? their newborn's named 'Apple'

Chrissy Hynde = deny she is rich…here is shiny CD

Christ the King = richest knight

Christina Aguilera = agile haircuts rain…uglier, Satanic hair…it is a raunchier gal...auric genital hairs...rage is a urinal itch...shag it in cruel aria...hail geriatric anus...rich girlie at sauna...agile haircuts rain...genital aura is rich...rich Italians argue...using clit hair area...an acute girlish air...I lag hair care units...I, a rich slut in a rage...I 'urt, achin' aria legs...hauls it in a carriage...rich aria gals unit

Christopher Columbus = such trip, such bloomer...cool ship's rum butcher...he is much corrupt slob...robs much, cruel to ship...curse much? or bolt ship...pilot's hombre such cur...clomb ship, hurt course...humblers occur to ship...such horrible top scum...rich problems touch US...Republic's mucho short...sub-tropic home's churl

Christopher Lee = strip leech hero...cheer this loper...cheer this prole...richer hole pest

Christopher Reeve = script: he ever hero...richest hoper ever...thrive creep horse?

CIA Director = adore critic...O dear, critic...dicier actor

Cindy Lauper = end up a lyric

Clancy Wiggum, Police Chief = icy, well-hung, comic pig-face

Cleopatra, Queen = eloquence apart

Cleopatra of Egypt = gal of top race type...great face, top ploy...got top pearly face...cap a plot, orgy, fete...plot a orgy, fete, Cap...people got a crafty

Antony and Cleopatra = only a ponce and a tart...act a one and only part...an annoyed, total crap

Clint Eastwood = Old West action...scowl antidote...lies down to act...low anecdotist...now eat clit, sod...a Old West tonic...to downscale it...O, wild act on set...Coda: won titles...a twisted colon

Clint Eastwood, the Actor = I do that cool Western act

Clint Eastwood, Film Producer = mid flop, re-edit, cut! won Oscar...prolific arts? women to cuddle...fit, old stud: Carmel power icon

Mr. Clint Eastwood = worst cinema dolt...I'd melt Oscar town...I'm actors' letdown...now, mildest actor...smart, townie clod...low domestic rant...I, most rated clown

Commissioner of Baseball = a fool slobbers, sane mimic...I'm a sane, if colorless bomb

Computer Scientist = I, rotten septic scum...inspect erotic smut...MIT: epic curse, so TNT...inept cost, curse MIT!

Condoleeza Rice = I concealed zero?...led zero cocaine?

Connie Francis = nicer fans' icon

Conservatives = craven Soviets

Constantine = ancient snot

Courtney Love = very cool tune...cool, true envy

Cristiano Ronaldo, Manchester United = so dance around team in Antichrist role

Dale Bozzio = I dazzle, boo!

Dallas Cheerleaders = elders sell a charade

Dan Aykroyd = a York dandy...do a dry yank...dry and okay

Dan Brown = own brand

Dan Brown, Writer of the Da Vinci Code = torrid wand of a bewitched conniver...I non-divorced benefactor withdraw...be convicted, if hot rod award winner

Da Vinci Code = candid voice...add vice icon

The Da Vinci Code = I'll have cited con...hectic video,

Dan…convicted, die, ha…do divine cachet…the candid voice…voiced an ethic…hat did conceive…did conceive, tah…voice hidden act…hidden voice, act…hidden act o' vice…had it conceived   addictive con, eh?

Danica Patrick = car-captain kid…acid antic, park…I'd panic a track

Danica Sue Patrick = pick a car and use it

Daniel Craig = I, darling ace…a girl can die…rancid agile…ice a darling

Daniel Craig, Actor = critic: a real gonad…cad in a tragic role…acting 'IRA cad' role…O, a critical danger

Daniel Craig, the British Actor = tail artistic high career: Bond…I, Bond chat: Hitler's a geriatric…rich attraction: he's bad, girlie…I slog in leading character…into this character, bad girlie?

Daniel Day-Lewis = is wild-eyed, anal…ideal lady swine…new ladies daily…idle ladies yawn…ideal, sinewy lad…I deny all we said…is indeed a wally…new lady is ideal?

Daniel Day-Lewis, the Actor = ideally, I wanted the Oscar

Daniel Gabriel Fahrenheit = infrangible heat dial here…I label heat here and in frig…I label infra-red heating, eh?

Daniel Ortega, President = top Red leader is in…I'd reign eternal…rein aged reinstated Pol

Dave Gahan = gave a hand…hang a deva

David Copperfield = VIP creep if odd lad

David Crosby, Solo If I Could Only Remember My Name = very dim fool, bald slob, cocaine's ruined my memory

David Crosby, Stephen Stills, Graham Nash, Neil Young = hey man, boring old c**ts sing shit verses all day, pah!

David Icke = advice kid

David Lee Roth = hot daredevil

David Letterman = terminal dead TV...nerd amid late TV...it darned, lame TV...evil dent mad art...vile end, mad tart

Dean Martin and Jerry Lewis = sad Italian 'n merry Jew nerd

Deceiver = received

Dennis Rodman = demon innards...in darn demons...odd man sinner...darn demon sin...odd in manners...and modern sin

Denzel Washington = zenith dangles now...long and tense whiz...England notes whiz...down angel's zenith

Designated Driver = danger is diverted...greater dividends

Detective Frank Serpico = present of creative dick

Diana Dors = as android

Princess Diana = *ascend in Paris...a car spin is end...dies in car, snap*...sad panic risen...car, snap, die, sin...pain as car's end...car ends as pain...I end as car spin...end is a car spin

Diana Frances Spencer = ascend Paris (en France)...a Press Dance in France

The Princess of Wales = ah, self-respect is won

Diana Spencer = nice snap, dear...Prince: a sedan...inane car sped...pain ends race...end race, pains...canned praise...a penis dancer

Princess Di = sic spin, red...spins, cried

The Prince of Wales = I, who left a Spencer...one epic Welsh fart...fine wet loser chap...a nit flower speech...wife's place: throne...if the Crown please...I place few thrones...can't feel his power...wasn't chief eloper...this welfare ponce...Charles wife, no pet...flew in, cop the ears...fleet-whores panic...loath wife: Spencer...O, he's perfect in-law?

Prince of Wales = crown if asleep

Prince Charles Windsor = princess, rancid howler...Crown pals, errs: Ich Dien...screw her rancid lips, no?

Camilla Rosemary Parker-Bowles = beware, a royal prick's more small...I am a merry raw bollocks pleaser...Balmoral pricks awesomely rare...was arse-licker, am royal problem...amiable porker screws amorally

Diana Ross = sans radio

Diane Keaton = take: do 'Annie'

Dick Clark = dark click

Dido (Florian Cloud de Bounevialle Armstrong) = so artful individual bloomed, record: 'No Angel'

Director of the CIA = oh, fierce dictator...it of retard choice...coo, terrific death...daft choice rioter

Dirty Old Man = randy, I'm told

Disraeli = I lead, sir

Doctor = cot rod...to cord

Doctor Dre = record dot

Doctor No = dot croon

Doctor Phil = pitch drool...old, top rich

Doctor Zhivago = void hog to czar

Dolly Parton = dyna-trollop...only part old...droll top? nay...top, only lard...on party doll

Donald Rumsfeld = meddler of lands…led old arms fund…slumland fodder…armed dolls fund…land of muddlers…dull and deforms…small DOD refund…me droll? add funds…smaller DOD fund?

Donald Rumsfeld, Defense Secretary = condescended elder, rule Army staff

Donald Trump = dump ton lard…mad old PR nut…turd palm Don…mad punt, Lord…Lord, damp nut…dump old rant…adult porn MD…damp old runt…told UN mad PR…odd rant lump…dolt ran? dump!

Donald John Trump = run, old phantom DJ…Lord, don't jump, nah…Jurmin Adolph, don't!

Donald and Melania Trump = putrid man and a mean doll…dull primate and Madonna

Donald Trump, President = it portends mad plunder…odd Mr. Putin's tender pal…prattle did upend norms…impudent plodders rant

President Trump = Mr. Putin's Red pet…printed up terms…sprinted up term…merit? ps: prudent

The Donald = old 'n hated

Donatien Aldonse Francois le Marquis de Sade = dear ladies' man and conquistadores felonies

Doubting Thomas = this good man, but

Douglas Adams = loud, mad sagas…Sago Mud salad

Dracula = a cur lad

Dracula, Prince of Darkness = snarl, sucker fancied a drop…undress crap, a naked frolic

Count Dracula, the Vampire = the valued, corrupt maniac

Count Dracula, the Famous Vampire = a human computer of vascular diet

Dr. Alois Alzheimer, the German Neurologist = memories going, lost in a rather dull…er…haze

Duke Ellington = liked long tune

Edward Kennedy Duke Ellington = wrinkled legend, odd Yankee nut

Dwayne Johnson = enjoys own hand

Dwight D. Eisenhower = now write, high deeds…God, white swineherd…wedding with heroes?

Dwight David Eisenhower = he did view the war doings…he hit and widows grieved

Earnest Hemingway = steaming anywhere…I'm nasty when eager…gem saint anywhere…yeah, new mastering…where nasty enigma?

Eddie Arcaro = I adored race…I odd ace, rare…ace dire road…I are odd race…ride ace road…a record idea…do a dire race

Eddie Fisher = if he desired

Eddie Murphy = I'm hyped, rude

Edgar Allan Poe = large lane dope…real lean dog, pa…pa, real lean god…Lord, a lean page…plan a large ode…ape and all gore…Lenore, a pal? gad

Edgar Poe = a God peer

Ed Roth = red-hot…the rod…he to dr.…he trod

Edward Teller = lewd, elder rat…well retarded…well, at red, red…relate lewd Dr.

Edward the Confessor = France's oddest whore

Ed Wood = odd woe

Elizabeth Taylor = O, her lazy able tit…ahoy! belle at Ritz…zero habit lately?

Elizabeth Taylor, Actress = total rich star, eyes blaze…eyes blaze, Christ to altar!

Miss Elizabeth Taylor = lazier, slimy, hot Beast

Liz Taylor = rot lazily

Elton John = let John on

Elvis = lives

Elvis Aaron Presley = seen alive? sorry pal…earns lovely praise…lives on as replayer

Elvis Aron Presley = on prayerless evil…evil, slayer person…yell as perversion…evil person layers…is slovenly Reaper…personally revise…lively, saner poser…lovelier siren sap…ol' prayer evilness…very painless role…prayer loveliness…in loyal preserves…in loveless prayer

Elvis Presley = lively sprees…verily sleeps…sleepy silver…silvery sleep…e'er sly pelvis…lisp severely…severely slip…pills ever? yes…severe sly lip…Presley Lives!

Elvis Costello = voice sells lot

Emerson Lake and Palmer = lend me Mark's aeroplane

Emperor = per Rome

Emperor Octavian = captain over Rome…ever a Roman topic…poor, creative man

Emperor of China = I'm arch foe prone…if cheaper moron…prime arch foe, no…chief rape moron…oh no, prime farce…prime arch foe, no?

Employee = yep, me, ole!

Engelbert Humperdinck = heckling perturbed man…gent RIP, number heckled…the number, legend, prick

Enrico Fermi = i.e. I'm for CERN!

Eric Clapton = narcoleptic…O, crap client…necrotic pal…I concert, pal…let crap icon…concerti pal…a lip concert…pencil actor…Plectra Icon…lip to cancer!

Esther Williams = as I'll swim there…I smell waterish

Evangelist = evil's agent

Ex-Husbands = shun bad sex

Exotic Dancers = nice sex act rod…can excite rods…do sex act nicer…concert aid, sex…sex act, cried: no…AC/DC exertions…concise: X-rated…excited acorns

Fantastic Four = act to ruffians

Fashion Designer = fine rig and shoes…fine rags on hides

Fashion Models = fool maids, hens…famished loons…do some flashin'

The Fashion Models = O, it handsome flesh…fleshiest manhood…the fool dishes man…flesh heads motion…a flesh on this mode'…this mode' flash one

Fats Domino = of saintdom

Federal Agent = a defter angel

Ferdinand Magellan = regal men find a land…large, damn, fine land…men find a large land

Fidel Castro = so daft relic…Red: it's focal…Florida sect…stolid farce…a Cold strife…docile farts…I scaled fort

First Lady = idly farts

The First Lady = has felt dirty...flirted hasty...shaft tiredly...flashy red tit...she, tad flirty...heard: tits fly!

Florence Nightingale = reflecting on healing...angel of the reclining...flit on, cheering angel...lice, filth, gangrene, no...fetch Nigel an iron leg...feel right on cleaning...hence I grant long life...ah, centering long life...a leg-leeching in front...I leech frontline gang...left Henri congealing...fetching linen galore...going, then clean rifle

Nurse Florence Nightingale = heroine curing fallen gents

Francis Scott Key = sanctify rockets...contacts fire sky...token fascist cry...crafts key tonic

Frank Frazetta = freak Tarzan ft.

Franklin Delano Roosevelt = vote for Landon 'ere all sink...love for Stalin, rankled one...no novel deal for real skint...not a novel deal for real skin

Fred Astaire = treader? as if...I tread safer...I, a sad ferret

Freddie and the Dreamers = er, dire, fans dreaded them

Freddie Mercury, the Queen Lead Singer = a quite rude, red-ringed felcher. yes, man...mere crude, sneering, filthy, dead queer

Friend = finder

Friends = finders...fend, sir

Frodo Baggins = bad ring's goof...bad ring goofs

Fundamentalist = fluent, mad saint...fluent mid Satan...nut flamed at sin

Galileo = I all ego

Galileo Galilei = agile illegal? Oi!

Galileo Galilei, the Italian Physicist = on a high Pisa, I elicit, tally legalities…on, a, Pisa, I elicit/tally high legalities

Gandalf = fag n' lad

Garbage Man = bag manager

Gary Condit = O trying cad…cryo-dating…at orgy in DC…ain't D.C. gory?

General Custer = curse Grant, Lee

General Michael Hayden = energy-man, he'll head CIA

Gene Roddenberry = greedy, boner nerd

George Bernard Shaw = abhorred, newer gags…rage, he's grown beard…rare, brown eggheads…grand, sober wag here…who renders garbage?

George Bush = he bugs Gore…sub hero egg…O, he buggers…ego bugs her…huge Gore BS…huge or begs…or begs huge…huge BS ogre

George Walker Bush = rake, who glubs beer…war geek ogre, blush…grow a beer keg lush…Hawk re-urges globe…Hawker urges globe…broke huge laws, regs…Hawk, beer-slugger…rule geek who brags…huge law go berserk…we're OK, beggar lush…bugger laws here, OK?

George Herbert Walker Bush = huge, berserk, rebel warthog

George Walker Bush, the President of the United States of America = takes power after foe, Mr. Clinton. but, gee, he's sure a shit-headed git…Empire State ego: he is a genuine bastard. f**k the rest of the world…debate it less. we ensure a gung-ho dictatorship of the Free Market…beguile workers' rights and attenuate *atheist* freedom of speech…seek bin Laden, he set out after Osama, forget it, he screwed right up…beef up U.S. oil interests, ah, shock and awe. thereafter, get Tom Ridge…he deregulates work to the edge. I hear fat-cat business profit…stop!

take Hitler: guess we see the huge, bad, reincarnated form of it...greed makes the habilitated terrorist thug use offence weapons...as war-games erupt, think of the benefit, get the dead oil resources...see doubted Chief kept in White House: *great letters for anagrams*...a total fascist buggered the U.S. I'm peed on weed, I shot the wanker...we see the fight to get Osama bin Laden, a sheer f**ked-up terrorist...beware! stupid ego gets set, makes a free land into the Fourth Reich...the obsessed, elite regretter. I'm a f**ked-up whore to Afghanistan...sleekest Saddam-hating newbie or the huge sputterer off erotica...the twit threatens Baghdad, to make sure of oil preference, I guess...guttersnipe emerges later, his father's a bonehead f**k-wit too...sweatiest geek of good putrefier: murder that Clint., he's a has been...he's the beast-like, fatuous faggot, he ordered war crimes. penitent?

George W. Bush, President = do sister, bugger nephew...the bigger power ends us...send the U.S. bigger power...South-bred n**gers weep...newest GOP greed: hubris...he pet, weird bugger's son...white person begrudges...enthused bigger powers...super-beings get whored...super Gore whinged best...purge those dweeb grins...pest in, buggered whores...buggered town sheep, sir...hreed grips the U.S., now beg

George W. Bush, President of the United States of America = won the race? Oh, bugger! I'm pissed off, attitudes are tense...see, the fag spied on us, he tortured a few Arabs in Git'mo, etc

President Bush of the USA = a fresh one, but he's stupid

Bush and Blair = a bland hubris...rubbish a land

George Clooney = cool energy ego...ER ecology? gone

George Harrison = hear gig and snore...hear singer and go

George Harrison, the Beatle = no bigger theatre arse hole

The Late George Harrison = singer: altogether a hero...O, he hot, great, real singer...Oh Ringo Starr, he legatee

George Lucas = oggler sauce...cruel ego gas...use C.G. galore...glucose rage

George Steinbrenner = serene, boring regent

George Washington = war on, he gets going...engaging to whores...reason, with eggnog...Oh, estranging we go...segregating now, Oh...a gent goes whoring...wig angers the goon...I, one ghost, anger G.W....ah, O, get ni**gers now!

Washington at Valley Forge = a few, they all go on starving

George Washington Carver = nigger saw North coverage

Gertrude Stein = registered nut

Gillian Anderson = alien's DNA on girl...no aliens, darling...aliens land on rig...and aliens on girl...long alien drains

Girlfriend = direr fling

Giselle Bundchen = nice blush legend...shine club legend...single nude belch

Gloria Estefan = large, fat noise...tale of a singer...no life as great

Gloria Steinem = male, ignores it...on girlie teams...in orgasm elite

Godfather = fat, red hog

Goethe = the ego

Golda Mier = E.G. I am Lord...old mirage...I'm real dog...Lord-image

Graham Nash = shh, anagram

Grateful Dead = dreadful gate

Great Scientist = nice strategist

Greg Rusedski = rugger kisser…drug geeks, sir…re: kiss rugger…Sir Geek Drugs

Greg Rusedski, Tennis Player = is seeking plenty rare drugs

Gustave Eiffel = gave us lift fee

Guy Fawkes = gawky fuse…few UK gays…wye UK fags…we UK fagys

Gypsy Rose Lee = 'e's sleepy orgy…sly eyes grope…yes, orgy peels…gory peels, yes?

Haley Joel Osment = ah, some jolly teen?

Harry James Potter = hey, pert, major star

Harry Potter = try hero part…harpy rotter…trophy rater

Helena Bonham Carter = no real charm beneath…be no ham, learn her act…hear her nobleman act

Helen Mirren, Actress = ER enters, lines charm…men relish screen art…isn't screen realm her?

Helen Mirren, the Actress = men relish the screen art

Actress Dame Helen Mirren = lead screen star? I'm her, men!

Henri Matisse = see, art's in him…is entire sham

Henry David Thoreau = another heavy Druid…a very hidden author

Henry Kissinger = King Henry lives!

Henry Miller = in merry hell

Hercules = he's cruel

Hermione Granger = ignore her German…renaming her Ogre…grr, heroine nag me

Heterosexual = a true sex hole...O her? use Latex...use extra hole...use ox leather...or he use Latex

Hillary Clinton = only I can thrill...lynch a trillion...lynch all in riot...all horny in clit...hy, Lincoln trail...I'l not lynch, liar!

Hillary Roddam Clinton = I'll anchor dirty old man

Hillary Rodham Clinton = lynch harlot in mid-oral...halt horny old criminal...I'd only thrill a monarch...Monica, horny-thrill lad...hi, a mad, rich nylon troll...trim lady anchor on Hill...halt horny old criminal...only I can troll him hard...chill nominator? hardly...Oo, damn richly in thrall...a myth-lorn child, no liar...drill: halt horny Monica...I chill on randy harlot M...Monica thrill horny lad...O mirth, hardly a Lincoln...an iron rhythmical doll...Hill myth or darn oilcan...all dry, thin old monarch...oil can harm idyll North...hid manly clitoral horn...no chlamydia or thrill...I normally hid, Charlton...chill, try 'n horde no mail...had matronly iron chill...crony dollar limit? nahh

Hillary Diane Rodham Clinton, Secretary of State = Anti-Christ mother really in decoy deal with Satan

Miss Hillary Rodham Clinton = his rich, slim lady: not normal...I'll marry childish man, O snot

Hippie = hi pipe

His Holiness the Pope = *he shits on his people*...ps: he is the Polish one...hint: hope is hopeless

Hollywood Agent = God, wealthy loon

Hollywood Hogan = hood? no, lowly hag

Homeowner = women hero...whore on me

Homer Simpson = mesomorph sin...posh misnomer...he romps in Mo's...Mrs. Homo Penis...ms. pre-homo sin...his prom's omen...no shrimps, Moe...me, sponsor him?

Homo Erectus = he rose to cum…costume hero

Housewife = use ho wife

Housewives = view houses

Howard Dean = he'd 'no war' ad…Dr. Ahead Now…dread won, ha…Oh, war 'n dread…Oh, a doctor waned

Howard Stern = wonder trash…nerd rat show…raw host nerd…ha, worst nerd…nerd who star…retard shown…star 'n whored…drew on trash…whored rants…sworn hatred…hater 'n words…strand whore…shorter wand…he drowns rat…we snort hard…raw Dr. Honest…nerd art show…worst and her…hard ten Sr, Ow…nerd star? how?

Humanitarian = I train a human…human in tiara…an am in a hurt

Husband = shun bad

Husband and Wife = fun was had in bed

Hustler = her slut

Humphrey Bogart = hyper thug Rambo…oh my, graph brute…grumpy hero bath…trophy bug harem

Idi Amin Dada = did aid mania

Iggy and the Stooges = they do onstage gigs…song they get is a dog

Ike and Tina Turner = ie: inane drunk tart…I entertain a drunk

Impotent Husband = humps not in/at bed

Iranian President = insane rant die, R.I.P.

Isaac Newton = was once a nit…now ace saint

Isaac Stern = a senarist…I, an actress…ace strains

Jackie Gleason = angelic as joke…agile jokes can…signal: ace joke…Angelica Jokes…align ace jokes…sale: ace joking…align joke case…c alien, joke gas

Jackie Mason = manic as joke…a manic jokes…maniac's joke…I'm a joke's can…joke in a scam

Jack Nicklaus = suck a Jacklin

Jake Lamotta = am take a jolt

James Bond = M, send a job

James Brown = Mr. Jawbones…jam on brews

James Brown, Godfather of Soul = adjustable whore go off norms

James Buchanan, President = the damn ____ bars Injun's peace

The Godfather of Soul = eh, he's a gruff, old toot…ugh, soft-hearted fool

James Cameron = major menaces…am major scene…major aces n' me

James Cameron, Director = set major cinema record

James Dean = a dense jam…made jeans

James Earl Carter, the Former President of the United States of America = rose from peanut farmer to a rich elder statesman: jet-setter, chief aide

James Fenimore Cooper = prose fee: major income

James Forrestal = star major feels…lest major fears…star major flees…jet, fears, morals…majors fear: 'lets'

James Vincent Forrestal = Majestic novel transfer

James Gandolfini = jail fine gods, man…lead Jingoism

fan…adjoining flames…joins if mad angel

James Madison, President = in a major mess? it depends

James Marshall Hendrix = hinder LAX, harmless jam…Shaman's hard remix jell…hard mixer, Shaman jells…hex jams Shaman driller…slim 'n relaxes, harsh jam

Jimi Hendrix = him dire jinx

James Scott Conners = connects major sets

Jimmy Conners = Jim 'n my censor…Mr. Joy 'n nice Ms.

James Taylor = oral majesty

Jane Seymour = sure joy, amen

Janet Jackson and Justin Timberlake = jubilant Satan jerks denim on jacket

Janet Reno = earn on jet

Jasha Heifetz, Violinist = join Liszt, achieve a shift

Jay Leno = enjoy LA

Jeane Dixon = a jinxed one

Jeff Bridges = Jr. begs, if fed

Jehovah's Witnesses = the Jewish son saves

Jennifer Aniston = fine in torn jeans…jeers in no infant

Jennifer Capriati = reject in fair pain…terrific Jane pain…inject, if rare pain…fair jet, nicer pain…jet, if in rare panic…I ran, if reject pain

Jennifer Lopez = jeer zone 'n flip…froze N.J. penile…jeez, felon 'n RIP…Jez, feline porn…Jez 'n fine prole…feel nip on jerz…elf in porn, jeez

Jennifer Love Hewitt = hint: evil O.J. went free…felt wet in her, no jive…thrive not, fine jewel

Jerome 'the Bus' Bettis = Oh Jesus, I'm better bet

Jerry Brown, Oakland Mayor = a badly jerky, narrow moron

Jerry Bruckheimer = rich jerk, mere bury…jerk, bury her crime…rich jerker bury me

Jerry Garcia = rare, racy jig

Jerry Seinfeld = friendly jeers…jeer if sly nerd…jeers are fiendly…fiendly Sr. Jeer

Seinfeld, US Comedian = audience fond smiles

Jerry Springer = grrr, spiny jeer…jee, grr, pry sin

Jerry Springer, talk show host = hapless jerk is not worthy, grr

Jerry Springer, television talk show host = joy? or sniveler twerps talking horseshit?

Gerald Norman Springer = nerd learning programs…gremlins arranged porn

Jesse Owens = seen Jew S.O.S.

Jesse the Body Ventura = jester behaves on duty…he enjoyed vast brutes…yes, adventure's the job…obey shaved jester nut

Jesus Christ = such jest, sir…JC thus rises…sh, just cries…riches 's just?

Jesus Christ and the Disciples = reject as stupid childishness?

Jim Brown = job: Mr. Win…obj: Mr. Win

Jim Marrs = I'm Mars jr.

Jim Morrison = Mr. Mojo Risin'

JK Rowling = low Jr. King…glow ink, jr….OK, win jr. gl…Jr. Owl King

Joe Biden = I need job…one jibes

Joe DiMaggio = amigo jog, die…I God, I jam ego…O, I'm aged jog…I God, I mega-Jo…I good age, Jim…I Jo, God-image…dig Joe, amigo…God, I Jo-image…I go aimed jog…I, doom-age jog…I jog a mad ego…Ji, I good game…I, amid ego, jog

Joe Namath = oh man, a Jet

Johannes Brahms, composer = he's major Bach sponsor, man

Johann Sebastian Bach = aha, enchantin' bass job

John Adams, President = jihad-mad person sent

John Belushi = eh, lush on job

John Elway = he lawn joy

John Kerry = horny jerk

Johnny Cochran = arch con Johnny

John Patrick McEnroe = chronic top-name jerk…arch jock, in? no temper?

John Paul Getty = thug planet joy

John Phillip Sousa = ah, so I push Joplin

John Ritter = Jr. in the rot…hotter in Jr.

John Ronald Reuel Tolkien = Ok, hell! jauntier Londoner

John Wayne = whoa Jenny!

John Wilkes Booth = blown his hot joke…*O, I know I shot LBJ*

Jon Anderson = Joann drones

Jonathan Frakes = ha, Jon's a Trek fan

JonBenet Ramsey = enjoy brat semen…enjoyment bears…enjoy 'n mere stab

Jon Heder = jo nerd, eh?

Joni Mitchell = joint chill me

Jose Canseco = Joe's con case

Jordan Nathaniel Marcel Knight = hot, entrancing, mad jerk in a hall

Judas = sad Ju

Judas Iscariot, the Disciple = I aid to epic lad: Jesus Christ

Judas Priest = just diapers

Judge Clarence Thomas = launch ejected orgasm

Judge Lance Ito = no, get Juide, lad

Judge Judy = J.J. guy dude?

Judy Garland = darn jug lady

Julia Roberts = I lust rear job…a sultrier job

Justin Bieber = ere just in bib…ebb injures it

Justine Henin = hi, June tennis

Justin Leonard = led, just an iron…lord, just inane

Justin Timberlake = I'm a jerk, but listen…tut, is a nimble jerk…brute? I'm Janet's ilk…I stumble, irk Janet…bum, tits, alien jerk…unstable jerk? I'm it…nut merit, likes a BJ…trim junkie bleats…l' make trust in J. Bie.

Kareem Jabbar = a jamb breaker

Karl Malden = all dark men

Kate Bush = shake but

Kate Moss = make toss…met ass, OK

Kate Winslet = wet tale, sink…sweet talkin'…new tits leak…taste winkle…le taste, wink

Kathie Lee Gifford = the glorified fake

Katie Couric = I cute, I croak

Katie Holmes = I am sleek, hot

Keith Moon = eh, I'm not OK…I'm OK, he not…the kimono

Keith Richards, the Rolling Stones Guitarist = the geriatric nihilist's on drugs, others talk

Keith Richards, Rolling Stones = his daring stoner's coke thrill…shit, girl, snort coke lines hard!

Kelly Ripa = pay killer…a perky ill

Ken Kesey = keen keys

Kevin Costner = sickener on TV…one sicker 'n TV

Kiera Knightly = large, kinky hit

Kind, Good-Hearted People = liken a good-deed prophet

King Arthur = hark, I grunt…I grunt: hark…hung rat, irk

King Arthur and the = ohh no, fit Dark Age thugs drink, battle, then run

Knights of the Round Table = Oh, King Artus felt the bond

King Hussein = nuke hissing…sink huge sin

King Henry the Eighth = think the high energy…hey, knight-thing here

Kirstie Alley = satire likely

Kissing Couples = spouses licking

Kitten Natividad = a kind, deviant tit…naked tit, avid nit

Kobe Bryant = nobby taker…betray nob…kabob entry

Kris Kristofferson = risk foreskin frost

Kurt Cobain = croak in tub…croak in but…OK, brain-cut…brain OK, cut…back to ruin…but a rockin'…backin' tour…a bit un-rock…a rockin' tub…boa in truck

Kurt Russell = truer Skulls…lust lurker…slut lurkers

Lady Gaga = a glad gay…gag a lady

Gaga = a gag

Ladies and Gentleman = England's elite and me

Lady of the Night = do the filthy nag

Laker Fans = near flasks

Laetitia Casta = ace as a tail, tit

Lance Armstrong = clear, strong man?

Lao Tsu = a lotus

Larry Flynt = try 'n all fry

Latoya Jackson = a nasal, jock toy

Lawrence of Arabia = Albion warfare ace…I balance era of war…I enforce a law, Arab…Arab wear facile, no?

Thomas Edward Lawrence = war was declared on them…had camels, drew no water…war wrath: deeds on camels…war-decorated Welshman…sand, camel, water: he'd row…who made desert clan war?

Thomas Edward Lawrence of Arabia = I saw he led Arab nomad force at war

Laura Bush, the First Lady = artfully hush brat's idea…as I artfully hushed brat…I bully a frustrated Shah…a tush Dubya rather fills

Laura Bush, the American First Lady = my husband, a hill creature, is a fart…US features a bandy Hill matriarch…husband, a rather mystical failure…family has created natural hubris…my husbands a rat! a Lucifer! a Hitler…I am after a cuter husband: Hillary's!

Laura Bush, First Lady = ah sir, study a full bra…Dubya's full hair star

Lawrence Olivier = cruel air, evil one

LeBron James = real men jobs…me learns job…jeer man, slob…mean LJ bores

Lebron Raymond James = modern joy realms: NBA…yes, male, born: M. Jordan

Lee Harvey Oswald = lay overhead, slew…revealed: who slay…lo, we've had slayer…so well-read heavy…a heavy, lewd loser…Reds have a yellow…a shy owl revealed…a sly deal, however…he was a lovely Red

Lee Marvin = eviler man

Len Bias = be slain…a, b, lines…ban lies…able sin

Leni Riefenstahl = senile Hitler fan…flash inner elite…The Infernal Lies…retains fine Hell…fine lies enthrall…neat fires in Hell

Lenny Bruce = runny celeb

Leonard Bernstein = rare blend in notes

Leonard Cohen = drone on, leach…hold an encore…a London cheer…cheer old anon…O lad, non-cheer…croon laden, eh?

Leonard Nimoy = I'm only a drone…dynamo in role…I led Moon yarn…I'm a loony nerd…on my alien rod

Mister Spock = prime stocks…me OK scripts…mocks priest…so Mr. Skeptic…smoke script…rest, I'm Spock

Leonardo Da Vinci = I'd carve on an idol…video on Cardinal…Vindaloo and rice…overlaid and icon…I'd novel can-do air…I drained volcano…advanced, or in oil…did color in a nave…I loved Draconian…Cardinal on video…and a divine color…an old, arid novice…O Draconian Devil…I drool in advance…cranial void done…an invalid Code, or…invalid acne door…a lover did con Ian…I carved on an idol…O, an invalid coder…loved in Rand. ciao!

Leonardo Da Vinci, the Artist Genius = Italian's hands receive tutor in God

Leonardo Da Vinci and His Paintings = I'd dig an inspiration held on canvas…an ancient passion did adorn living, ah…ah, can land God's divine inspiration

Leonardo DiCaprio = ocean idol or a drip…O, paranoid Ice Lord…docile or paranoid

Leper = repel

Lev Nikolaevich Tolstoy = O, it's a lovely thick novel

Liberal Democrats = a terrible, old scam…merited local bars…crime-deal: Borstal…dismal career-blot…miserable, cold rat…dream bill to scare…arm electoral bids…liars led, mob react…Blair electors: mad…creditable morals…all mediocre brats…dismal, rectal bore

Libertarian = retail brain

Lieutenant = an elite nut…i.e. untalented…until eaten

Linda Lovelace = clean, vile load…all clean video…loved alliance?

Lindsay Davenport = adv' tennis-pro lady…av'd tennis-pro lady…a prov'd tennis-lady

Lisa Simpson = so plain miss…slim passion?

Literary Agent = rate ingrately…a gentle rarity…in early target…ingrately tear…generality rat…great, arty line…retain greatly…generality art…it nearly great…early treating…angry, elite rat

Literary Agents = tales are trying…strange reality

Little Richard = a direct thrill

Lleyton Hewitt = hit net, yowl: 'let'…newly hot title…the lonely twit…why little note?

Lorne Michaels = clean, slim hero…is romance hell…eh, smaller icon…hell, I'm a censor…censorial helm…ahem, nice rolls…small, nice hero?

Louis Daniel Armstrong = an ideal monstrous girl…a minstrel and glorious…old arms, original tunes…sound art, a smiling role…so I'm an ultra-old singer

Lucianno Pavarotti = ultra-ovation panic…crap ovational unit

Ludwig Van Beethoven = ugh, new involved beat…Vienna vet who bugled…tuba legend when vivo…loved having new tube…a debut when evolving

Lyndon Baines Johnson = so ninny handles job? no!

Macaulay Culkin = I am a luck lunacy

Madonna = and moan…don a man…'n do a man

Madonna Ciccone = c'mon, a dance icon

Madonna Louise Ciccone = one cool dance musician…occasional nude income…iconic cones? a loud amen…anomalous coincidence…unsocial, demon cocaine…canoodle one musician…once unsocial comedian…uncool as nice comedian…cool, ace, nude insomniac…I am a conscience on loud…no, I am a loud conscience…ideal scum on, on cocaine…no ideal scum on cocaine…an economic, social nude…canoodle on a nice music…cosmic audience on loan…unsocial code, mean icon…is uncool menace on acid…cool, so nude, nice maniac…is cool audience con man

Mae West = am sweet…sweat me…sew mate…Sweet Ma…wet as me…waste me…we mates…wet seam…we steam

Mamie Van Doren = a drive, men moan…I'm a raven demon…and I am over men

Mao Tse Tung = tame, no guts…must not age…mutant's ego…to get us, man

Mao Tse Tung, Chairman = a great Communist? nah…utmost China manager…man's truth: egomaniac…mutant American hogs…met us on a giant march…act got human remains…not China-master, a mug…most argute Chairman

Chairman Mao = I am on a march…I am a monarch

Marc Bolan = BLAM! no car…lamb in car…normal cab…carnal mob

Marcello Mastroianni = romantic, manlier also…I'm also Latin romancer…actor's realm in Milano

Marcia Clark = am crack liar

Marco Polo = a cool romp

Mark McGwire = I'm a wreck mgr.

Madame Curie = me, radium ace

Marie Curie = re: aim, I cure…I cure a mire…me, I cure air

Maria Schneider, Actress = character's arse is mined

Maria Sharapova, Tennis Player = am a pain as trophy rival, Serena?

Maria Sharapova, Wimbledon Champion = I am a Siberian vamp who can hold a romp

Marie Antoinette = one in a trim-a-tete…a termination tee…terminate on a tie…mention "eat," irate

Margaret Thatcher = that great charmer…grrr, a hatchet, mate…charm great threat…the great charm rat

Marge Simpson = so prim, nags me…orgasm, spin me…penis'm, orgasm…is pro men's mag…re: mom, gasp, sin…Miss Mega-Porn?

Mariah Carey = a creamy hair…ah, creamy air…hairy camera…I am racy, hear?

Marijuana Dealer = jeer a manual raid…damn jail, rue area…unarmed jail area

Marilyn Manson = many sin, normal…Roman manly sin…Ms. Amoral Ninny…manly man? no, sir…my norm, anal sin

Marilyn Monroe = in lore, my Norma…many minor role…I marry loon men…marry no oilmen…moral irony: men…moan on merrily…I'm nearly moron…learn in my room

Marilyn Monroe, Cinema Star = many men's amoral criterion

Marine Biologist = I'm boring sea toil

Mark Chapman = pack harm man…harm Pack-Man

Mark Cuban = muck'n Arab…a numb rack…a crank bum

Mark Hamill = I'm hallmark

Mark Spitz = task: Mr. Zip

Mark Twain = am rank wit

Samuel Clemens = clueless man, me

Marlene Dietrich = nice Hitler dream…I'd leer at rich men…reel charm in edit…cinema hit, Dr. Leer

Marlon Brando = born, moan, lard…abnormal? No Dr….Roman born lad…London bar ram…drab, non-moral?

Brando, the Movie Legend = big role and Method, even

Marquis de Sade = is masqueraded…queer, sad maids

Marshall Mathers = small hater's harm…harm, mash, sell art…rather small sham…small trash harem

Martha Stewart = master at wrath!

Martina Navratilova = variant rival to a man…valiant Moravian rat…O man, a vain rival tart…am valiant or variant…vain, vain, amoral tart

Martin Gore = organ merit…great minor…organ timer…I'm torn rage…I term organ…German riot…a grim tenor…Roman tiger

Martin Luther = manlier truth…terminal hurt…truth in Realm…I'm learn truth…truth: men: liar…Mr. in the ultra…Mr. Alien Truth…I'm alert 'n hurt…I'm renal truth…I'm real 'n truth…ram truth line…I'm t' renal hurt…ram Hitler-nut…liar, truth 'n me…truth mar line…hurt men trial…mirth: neutral…I'm Hun rattler

Martin Luther King Junior = mini truth learing or junk?

Dr. Martin Luther King, the Late, Great = a dreamer greeting truth, think tall!

Martin Scorsese = I scare monsters…romances sister…screen is a storm

Martin Sheen = Shite manner…am the sinner…intense harm

Mary Kay Letourneau = amour? nay, a tyke lure

Mary Lou Retton = O, manly torture

Mary Magdalene = my, am dear angel…a randy lame gem…am dreamy angel…am, am legendary…'n eagerly madam…near legy madam

Mary Pierce = pricey mare

Mary Queen of Scots = O fear my conquests…fame conquers toys…steamy of conquers

Mary Wollstonecraft Shelley = hey, tall fellow, scary monster!

Mata Hari = ha, I'm a rat

Mats Wilander = wasn't Mr. Ideal…trawl maidens…last weird man

Matt Damon = madman tot…am damn tot

Matt Groening = get mint organ

Matthew Perry = wrathy temper

Matt Leinart = a trim talent…it mental art…it arm talent…metal, tin rat…tart ailment…it, Ram talent

Maurits Cornelis Escher = semi-circular otherness

Max Schreck = Marx checks

Meg Ryan = Germany…my anger…Eng. Army…Mary Eng.…nay germ…yarn gem…gray men…grey man…army gen.…me gay R.N…any germ…angry? me?

Melanie Griffith = right fee in a film

Mel Gibson = bong smile...bong slime...big melons...limbs gone...big, solemn...glib omens...snog me, lib

Meryl Streep = me, reply? Rest

Mary Louise Streep = your merit pleases...supreme royalties...a mysterious leper?

Michael Bolton = I'm the local nob

Michael Caine = I am a nice lech...I'm a nice leach...I license a ham...a He-Man icicle...i.e. mechanical...I, a name cliché...a lice machine

Michael Caine, Actor = I cheer acclamation...I'm a laconic cheater...I am a central choice...ach, a cinema role...mechanical erotica...heroical cinema act...I catch a cinema role...a nice Croat: A Michel...a chemical reaction...reaction: acclaim, eh?

Michael Caine, the Actor = choice theatrical name...real choice that cinema...the ham actor in Cecelia...cliché: ham actor, nae tie

Sir Michael Caine, Actor = as a rich, cinematic role...O, a ham, a critic silencer...I acclaim neither Oscar...acclaim in either Oscar

Michael Collins, the Astronaut = it's Moon launches that I recall

Michael Dukakis = like a dim U.S. hack

Michael Gough = magic ghoul, eh?

Michael Jackson = manacle his jock...manic joke clash...hijack calm nose...he's jail cock man...moans, jail cock...conk jail schema

Michael Jackson, Pop Star = special jockstrap, oh man

Michael Jackson, the Pop Singer Dies = leading act perishes, no chimp jokes

Michael Jordan = idol, can jam her…hero clad in jam…Jam on, rich deal…charm jailed, no…hid clean major…March, no jailed

Michael Keaton = I am a token lech…the coke animal…mean, OK, ethical

Michael Landon = I am old channel…hi, clean, old man…clean mind halo

Michael Richards = held a rich racism…hear racism, child?

Michael Shermer = shh! mere miracle…he, Slime Charmer…me, smirch healer…hmm, lie-research?

Michelangelo = manic ego hell

Michelangelo Buonarroti = machine-tooling labourer…oh, cut one original marble…learn in both: image, color…honorable, romantic guile

Michel De Nostradame = the demonical dreams…I'm a demented scholar…this old dream menace…old man's made heretic…had time-clone dreams…he meant: odder claims…Alchemist dreamed on…let him dream a second…heed modal miscreant…halo determined scam…this dream: old menace…old man made heretics…the mind made oracles…search and model time…oracle shed damn time…oracles? I demand them…clear mind do the same

Michel De Nostradamus = on dreams: much detail…I dreamt such omens, lad…aim? damned short clues…random items had clues…he admits: 'random clues'

Nostradamus = man soars! Utd….do Sun, Mars, ta…roast us? damn…mad or as nuts…USA and storm…USA 'n stardom…sound at Mars…O, dramas stun…us, a smart nod…astound Mars!

Nostradamus, French Physician and Astrologer = predicts floods, arm using an anarchy on Earth

Michelle Obama = I'm a macho belle…ah, libel ace mom?

Michelle Obama, First Lady = I + BHO created small family…Lord, I am a sly female bitch…the old America falls, I'm by…billed a star, chiefly a mom…model shift by all America…sly chief mom: a tad liberal…hi, my fella's a lib Democrat…I'm Michael Flatley's broad

Michelle Obama, the First Lady = *female balls,* hey: him dictator

Michelle Obama Purpose = secure impalpable *homo*

Mickey Mantle = tickle my mane…meanly tick me

Micky Dolenz = monkied lecz

Miguel Cervantes de Saavedra = gave us a damned clever satire…I'm savage, adventure declares

Mike Tyson = sit, monkey…yo, me stink…KOs enmity

Mikhail Gorbachev = a cover, KGB hail him…I charm, ah, I love KGB

Miley Cyrus = use my lyric…yes, I'm curly…lyric, um, yes…cry, "Elysium"

Miss Miley Cyrus = my muse is lyrics

Millionaire = limo, airlines…oil liar in me…oil rain mile…I'm in real oil

Miss Moneypenny = men spy, my one sin…M's spyin' on enemy

Mister King Camp Gillette, the Inventor = shaving torture? I permit gentle tickle

Moebius = Oi, e's bum?

Moe Szyslak = lazy, smokes

Mohammed Ali = maim mad hole…modal maim, eh…I'm made,

halo me...oh, I'm mad, lame

Monica Lewinsky = lo, my wank is nice...I cosily wank men...I mean slinky cow...seminal now icky...I yen, woman licks...knew a slimy icon...a lick on my swine...knows I'm nice lay...money was in lick...a lick wins money...now I lay sick men...coy, seminal wink...say: lick mine now...wank my silicone...my known CIA lies...ow, my insane lick...we may lock in sin...news may coil ink...nice silky woman...a lick on my sinew...Slick in me? no way...Slick may win one...slinky ice woman...a nice snowy milk...now lie in my sack...I wink, Sly came on

Monica Samille Lewinsky = Slick Willie's my A-one man...sick woman lies menially...well, my sick liaison, amen...sickly Willie moans, amen...I see silly woman lick man

White House Intern Miss Monica Samille Lewinsky = I'm newsworthy, semi-senile humiliation slackens...hi, hey, William Clinton arouses me, I'm Ken's witness

Monica, Beverly Hills = Bill can, he is my lover

Monica Seles = smiles on ace...I'm ace lesson...so mean slice...sales, income...camel noises...a comeliness

Montgomery Cliff = comfortingly fem...off-girly comment...confirm lofty gem

Morgan Fairchild = if rich and glamour...am darling of rich...do charming flair...rich foam, darling

Morrissey = is so merry

Mother-In-Law = *woman Hitler*

Mussolini = I'm sin soul...minis soul

Benito Mussolini = built noisome sin...bum's notion is lie...mob unionist lies

Nadia Comaneci = I am ace and icon...I'm an ace on acid...I am a dancer icon…no academician

Nancy Kerrigan = grace 'n any rink

Tonya Harding = grand hit on ya…do an angry hit…hit, darn agony

Naomi Watts = a tits woman

Napoleon Bonaparte = no, not appear on Elba…no, a trap open on Elba

Natalie Portman = I am porn talent…not a Parliament…an animal potter

Native Americans = I am a nice servant…is variant menace

Nat King Cole, the Singer = sang nice, gentler hit OK…thinking: elegant score

Neil Diamond = no ideal mind…I'm an odd line…oldie man, din…inlaid demon…Indian model

Neil Young = online guy

Nelson Mandela = lean and solemn…a non-small need

New Kids on the Block = now kicks the blonde

New Kids on the Block, the Boy Band = think back: they'd be old bones now

Newt Gingrich = wrenching git

Leroy Newton Gingrich = right-winger only once…yon right-winger clone…growing incoherently…grow incoherent lying

Niccolo Machiavelli = evil, manic alcoholic

Nick Lachey = lay chicken

Nicola Tesla = allocate sin…locale saint…clean to ails…is a

Lancelot...ace stallion...is on tall ace...is neat local...stoical al'en...lean, stoical...a tall cosine...l'asocial ten...tall, ace ions...an oscillate...can steal oil...a still ocean...last ace lion...scale, no tail

Nikola Tesla = take all ions...last alien, OK...talk so alien...alias: ol' Kent...O, alien talks...ask alien, lot...I takes on all...it a son, Kal-El...to Kal aliens...kill, ate a Son...Atlas 'n OK lie...OK, let's a nail...I OK: tall, sane...talk as no lie...I talks alone...a kill on a set...OK, slain tale...late, slain, OK...O, a neat skill...alien talk so...so, talk alien...no like Atlas?

Nikola Tesla, the Inventor = kilovolt antenna? it's here!

Nicole Kidman = a demonic link...I'm a kind clone...I'm no clean kid

Nikita Khrushchev = shhh, nuke via trick

Noel Coward Is = no Oscar Wilde

Noel David Redding, the late bass guitarist of the Jimi Hendrix Experience = just a sex-mad ginger, afro-head, indecent, exhibitionist pervert: hell, I died!

Noel Redding, Bassist = tangible sordidness

Norman Bates and His Mother = HE'S the madman on brains rot

North American Indian = harm and incineration...I'm reincarnation hand

Norwegians = Swen or Inga?

Nuclear Physicists = sun-star cycle is hip...psychiatric, unless

Oliver North = thorn or evil...evil horn rot

Oliver Reed = erode liver...ode re: liver...eviler doer

Oliver Stone = sore, violent

Oliver Wendell Holmes = he'll do in mellow verse

Olivia = via oil

Oprah Winfrey = hype worn fair...pay for whiner...for when I pray

Orenthal James Simpson = OJ, he Seminal sportsman...host OJ, primal meanness...Mr. OJ, meanness hospital...OJ, immense sharp talons...Heisman plot, snare Ms. OJ...moonlit James sharpens...immense harlot, OJ snaps...OJ slashes prominent ma...Heisman person jolts ma...inept OJ slashes mom, ran...OJ, him last mansion spree...Ms. OJ's Ron, lame thespian...I'm OJ, slashes neat Ron, PM...hapless Ron join tame Ms....patrolmen hiss OJ's name...ashen patrolmen miss OJ...jam, solemn Shapiro sent...Shapiro menses jolt man...OJ's solemn, Marsha inept...Ron set OJ, Heisman plasm...OJ, less mama, then prison

Orson Welles = now roleless...now reel loss

Osama = as Mao

Osama bin Laden = a damn alien SOB...is a banal demon...abandon a smile...old man in a base...a noble man said...led, O, I'm bananas...an Islam bad one...a bad, neon Islam...an old, mean bias...an ode: ban Islam...I, bananas model...bad as Lenin, Mao...I am also banned...noble, mad Asian...bold, mean Asian...I, a damnable son...O, a damnable sin...so bad, alien man...a mad, inane slob...a nomad lesbian...O, damn, a lesbian...O, insanable mad...maiden on a slab...bad also in name...is an able nomad...based on animal...bad as mean lion...bad man is alone...O, anal, sad bi-men...in a mad one's lab...a bad man, (no lies)...I, bad man on sale...so die, banal man...O, banal man dies...a dismal bane, no?

The Terrorist Osama Bin Laden = Arab monster is no idle threat...I'm a total abhorrent direness...a Hitler or so eminent bastard...Beast in error, don't hate Islam...snide bat, Hitler, Satan or more...a tormented Satan is horrible...the dirtiest abnormal reason...no more trials bathed in tears...a dishonorable treatment, sir…this rotten Arab is real demon…the stolider Arabian monster…a silent, horrid Arab sent to me…so, a mortal brain in the desert…so he's a terrible dirt, not a man…hate on Blair in a 'Desert Storm'…that error is to be mad as Lenin…be death, mortal sin is not rare…listen, a horrid Arab sent to me…terminate dishonorable rats…this, a demon or terrible Satan…this means a terrible tornado…seen this, Lord? I'm a rotten Arab…another lie? no, Mister Bastard…dear, this rotten animal bores…this rotten Arab soldier, amen

Terrorist Osama Bin Laden = Islam's obedient narrator…no, Islam's dire, rotten Arab…no, a terrible mad arsonist…arsonist named liberator…morals? none, dirtiest Arab…rotten Arab morals inside…I'm Satan's bloodier ranter…Satan's terrible, main odor…Satan's tidier, abler moron…I'm a noble, arsonist retard…Arab arsonist melted iron…Beast or maladroit sinner…aberrant, Islam-rooted sin…arson-oriented Islam brat…rotten brain adores Islam…bloodier, insane, smart rat…Islam's rodent aberration…a balmier, arsonist rodent…Oi, Islam's aberrant rodent…Oi, Islam's rotten nerd Arab

Oscar Wilde = I lace words…ladies crow

Osiris = or Isis

Ozzy Osbourne = boozy nor Zeus…no sober, you ZZ…O, one rosy buzz

Pablo Casals, Cellist = I'll clap to bass scale…top classic labels

The Late Pablo Casals = that, a passable cello

Pablo Picasso = pop, basic also

Palestine Liberation Organization = I go plot a riot in Israel, an insane bet?

Palestinians = plain nasties…it's insane, pal

The Palestinians = let pain in the ass?

The Palestinian Soldier = spin line: *Death to Israel!*

Palestinian Terrorists = it is not Israel's partner...intent? Israel's airports...airport's trials intense...it so Israel isn't partner...rapists in eternal riots...sinister, nastier patrol...non-literate rapists, sir...Israel's irritant pest, no?

Pamela Anderson = adores men, a plan...porn as mean deal...O man, laden pears...a darn, ample ones...melons and a pear...mean personal ad

Pam Grier = grim rape

Paramedic = came rapid

Paris Hilton = rat in polish...posh, tin liar

Pat McEnroe = compare net

Patrick Rafter = far, racket trip

Patrick Stewart = a crap Trek twist...act as Trek twirp

The English Actor Patrick Stewart = he's captain to Star Trek crew, light

Paul McCartney = pay Mr. Clean-Cut...um, cancel party...crap met lunacy...campy Uncle Art...pay calmer c**ts

Sir Paul McCartney = crap musical entry...man captures lyric...musical carpentry...a clean, prim, crusty

Paul Michael Glaser = ace phallus, I'm huge!

Paul Robeson = blue soprano

Paul Stanley = yell up Satan...ya, plane lust...a lusty plane...any pale slut

Paul Winchell, the Ventriloquist = voice talent will then hurl quips

Peabo Bryson = snobby opera

Peggy Fleming = Peg: flying gem

Penn and Teller = repellant 'n end

Peter Allen = an repellent

Peter Cushing = thug creeps in…upright scene…I grunt speech

Peter Frampton = perform patent

Peter Jackson, Hobbit Trilogy Film Director = copied JRR Tolkien's right crafty Bilbo, to me

Peter Lawford = reported flaw

Peter Max = am expert

Peter North = tether porn…re: pert 'n hot…pert hornet…potent Herr…pert throne…rotten herp

Peter O'Toole = reel poet too

Peter, Paul and Mary = play a drum 'n repeat

Peter Ustinov = one truest VIP…to purest vein…eruptive tons…step on virtue

Pete Sampras = repeat spasm

Pete Townshend = end: WHO, net pest

Pet Shop Boys = they pop sobs

The Pet Shop Boys = both soppy, these

Phil Jackson = his jock plan

Phil Mickelson = limp nick holes…skill chip on me…hi, compel links…no chip kills me…chops link mile…chop skill in me…chip, mole, links…hell, I'm skin cop

Philo Farnsworth = whir proton flash…whirls photon far

Pierce Brosnan = borne as Prince…inborn as creep…prancer, i.e. snob

Pierre-Auguste Renoir = I err, re-use rouge paint

Piet Mondrian = I paint modern

Plato = a plot

Playmate of the Year = ahoy, a pretty female…hey, a top arty female

Pocahontas and John Smith = champs join hands to patch a nation…Jamaican snapshot and in hotchpot

Politician = I, in Capitol…I nail topic

Politicians = topical is in…is in Capitol…solicit pain…in social pit…lip is action…I, action lips…I optical sin

Pontius Pilate = up polite saint…up its top alien…it pole up saint…so title, up pain…up saint to pile…I neat populist…saint it up pole…slept in utopia

Pope John Paul, His Holiness = hope in Polish plan, Oh Jesus!

Pope John Paul, the Second = happen-so, the jocund Pole

Popes and Archbishops = bad, cheap sponsorship

Postman = no stamp

Pot Dealer = dope alert…later, dope…top leader

Psychopath = chops thy pa

President Putin of Russia = in future, stops in despair

Putin, the President of Russia = I punish deepest frustration…in the future, stops in despair…super fine dirt up into the ass…porn input satisfied the user...often stupid, is near pure shit...this pure, nude artist of penis...a definite truth suppression...he is a super student in profit...put the perfidiousness in art

Vladimir Putin, the Russian President = devilish, imprudent, nastier Rasputin...punitive triumpher in dastardliness...unvaliant, shittier, dried-up primrose

Vladimir Putin, President of Russia = vast Imperialist ruin, de profundis...first master in individual purpose...viperous Stalinism if prurient dad

Vladimir Putin, President = imp, turd: privatized Lenin...evil-minded Rasputin trip...

President of Russia = iron-fisted, USSR ape...satisfied porn user...persuasion? Red fist!

The President of Russia = Putin, hardest foe, rises...fears the Putin dossier...sheer disaster of Putin

Russian President Putin = Rasputin intrudes penis

Prince = nice PR

The Artist Formerly Known as Prince = no first rate workmanship recently...so rich talent now prefers tiny mark...tiny, short freak relents: "I'm crap now"...foreskin chewer rants importantly...terrific man spanks whore rottenly...terrific, warm, nasty, honest plonker...the wrinkly transformations creep...sorry prick with mere fans, no talent

Prince Andrew, Duke of York = randy wife round pecker, OK...Yank porked cruder wife, no?

Prince Phillip, the Duke of Edinburgh = hope I'd help future King pinch a bride

HRH Prince Phillip, Duke of Edinburgh = huh, high-priced, inbred plonker, if up

The Duke of Edinburgh = though drunk, I beefed…he'd find tough rebuke…if Greek, he'd doubt Hun…Oh, but he'd dunk Fergie…fine, but odd Greek, huh?

Princess Margaret = crap German sister

Prometheus = the Supremo…me super hot…hot supreme…presume hot

Prostitute = tourist pet…spitter-out…true to spit…pet out tits

Queen Elizabeth, the First = her bequest: life at zenith!

Queen Elizabeth, the Second = a zest behind the eloquence…I squeeze the noble hand, etc…sleaze? do quieten the bench…not equalized, hence behest…she'd be eloquence at zenith…not end the sizable cheque

Queen Isabella of Spain = I ban sea fellas: no equip

Queen Latifah = hail, fat queen

Queen Mother = hot, queer men

Queen Victoria = I antique cover…I vainer coquet…O, I quite craven…to acquire vein…I quit Care Oven…Care Oven, I quit…I've no care, quit…I've quite car, no?

Victoria, the Queen = no quiet here at Vic…inactive, hot *queer*

Quetzalcoatl = Aztec quota ll

Rafael Nadal = a dear fan, all…a real fan lad…a dear 'n a fall

Ralph Nader = plan harder…ran, held par…hear plan Dr.

Ralph Waldo Emerson = person whom all read

Ramone Navarro = ran over a Roman…or ran over a man…rare, Roman nova…or Roman era van…roam on rare van…overran a Roman…on a Roman raver

Rand McNally = Mr. Clay N. Land…manly land, c.r.

Rape Victim = it cream VIP

Raymond Burr = brandy rumor

Red Hot Chili Peppers = tip: shred rich people…their crippled hopes

Reggie Bush = gee, big rush…us, he bigger…he big surge…'Bus' gig here…big urges, eh…is huge berg…Heis bugger…I be egg rush…ge, huge ribs

Regis Philbin = hire glib spin

Research Scientist = hire, tests nice cars

Restauranteur = rare, utter anus…tuna treasurer…rat nature? sure

Richard Attenborough = hurrah to bored acting

Sir Richard Attenborough = honour graced British art

Richard Branson = baron's darn rich

Richard Hoagland = halo and arch grid

Richard Milhouse Nixon = climax ruined his honour…climax is hinder honour…is human, horrid lexicon…innoxious child harmer…in unheroic Marx in hold

Richard Starkey = rather scary kid…shy, dark, erratic

Richard Widmark = I'm dark, rich draw

Ridley Scott = dirty closet…cry: "let's do it!"…costly, tired

Rik Ocasek = I rock sake

River Phoenix = X heroin Viper…X-hero in Viper…I, X-hero vein PR…O, rip vein, her X…oh, Rex in Viper…oh, rip vein, Rex…rip vein or hex…or hex in Viper…pix or her vein…vein hero prix...prior vein hex...rev, pix heroin...Rex heroin VIP...heroin vex, R.I.P...I've X-heroin PR...no hire Rex VIP...no hirer ex-VIP...ex heir, nor VIP...oh, expire in RV...expire nor HIV

Robbie Williams = I will arse bimbo

Roberta Pedon = top boner, dear...bet: adorn porn...on top, rare bed...bored, eat, porn...report on a bed...predator bone...one bad report...taped or boner...O dear, porn bet...bare torn dope...O dear, pert nob...porn or debate...dope 'n aborter

Robert Blake = barrel OK bet...OK rebel brat

Robert Dinero = error on bidet

Robert Francis Kennedy = rednecks bore infantry

Robert Louis Stevenson = novelist's true bore, son...not so subservient role

Roberto Duran = round aborter...round rat bore...adore or burnt...adorn or brute...a true-born rod

Robert Plant = nob prattler

Robert Redford = Bedford terror

Robin = borin'

Robin Williams = I warm billions...in similar blow...simian bill row

Rock Hudson = shock round...oh no, suck Dr.

Rod Laver = old raver...rover lad...overlard

Rod Serling = Lord singer

Rod Stewart = worst dater...rated worst

Roger Federer = error-free ged...freer or greed...error-free edg'…degree for err…grr, do referee

Roger Federer, the Swiss Tennis Player = error-free swing, sharp-eyed, tests line

Roger Waters = regrets a row

Ronald McDonald = droll conman, dad…darn cold, old man

Ronald Reagan = an oral danger…adrenal groan…learn a dragon

Ronald Wilson Reagan = no darlings, no ERA law…a lone insane warlord…insane Anglo warlord…now a gnarled liar, son…so grand an Orwellian…goal now: slander Iran…a warning, an old loser…land owner's oral gain

Ron Jeremy = re: Mr. Enjoy…Mr. Enjoyer

Ron Paul = our plan

Rothschild = hold Christ…sh, told rich…hitchs Lord…hitch Lords…rich, hot LSD

The Rothschild = hot Christ, held

Roscoe Fatty Arbuckle = cocky-sure of able tart

Ross Martin = minor stars

Rowan Atkinson = Anorak Winston…wanks, not on air…raw onion stank…isn't anorak now

Royalty = Tory lay

The Royal Family = I hefty amorally…tally-ho, May fire…eh, fly amorally...a real filthy, O my…I am Earthly folly…tally-ho, am fiery…tally-ho, me fairy…my faith, O really…if a motherly lay…they if amorally…if harem loyalty…'The Firm,' ya loyal?

Roy Scheider = hide sorcery

Rudolph Valentino = uh, top lover in land…thud, love-lorn pain…pin unloved harlot…hold up, no interval…love-lorn and up hit

Rudyard Kipling = I gulp a drink dry

Rudy Giuliani = I aid ugly ruin…I dig unruly, Ai!

Rush Limbaugh = I harm lush bug…sh, humbug liar…ha, glum hubris

Russell Crowe = Orwell's curse…slower ulcers

Rutger Hauer = the rare guru

Ryan Seacrest = necessary rat

Ryuichi Sakamoto = I'm such a riot, okay?

Saddam Hussein = has nudes, maids…ass! humans died…UN's said he's mad…I had U.S. madness…hides, damns USA…dead in U.S. smash…USA ends him, sad…hissed: damn USA…him saddens USA

Saddam Hussein, President = human disaster dispensed…damn! diseased penis hurts…super sadism ends in death…ended, assassin triumphed…pinheadedness, sadist, rum…a surest, pissed, hidden man…stupid and denser messiah…undesired spasm in death…death spider madness in us…dream ends in US death, piss…mad rat, he despised Sunnis…hands up, Media dissenters…serpent, mad Hun is sad, dies…he ran: dies, stupid madness…as rude man, dispensed shit…Saddhu meanspiritedness…dread nemesis tips US hand…unarmed, and despises this…a punishment is addressed…this means sudden despair…intended mishaps assured…and here is stupid madness…damn! he's a super dissident…miser, he stands up and dies…Putin dreams his deadness…sad pride, madness in US…this dried-up, mad saneness…hides madness in used trap…this is Superman's dead end…sins, ha! sudden trap demise…ashamed, putrid snideness…shredded supine Satanism…undesired spasms in death…miser, he stands up and dies…ends, is this Superman dead?

Saint John the Baptist = atheist's job in N.T. path

Salesman = nameless

Salman Rushdie = read, shun Islam

Salvador Dali = Avida dollars

Sam Cooke = makes coo

Sam Elliott = total slime

Sam Snead = a madness

Samuel L. Jackson = so small ace, jink

Samuel Taylor Coleridge = gloom led literary cause...O great, musical yodeler

Samurai Warrior = is raw armour air

Sandra Bullock = Skull and Cobra

Sargent = strange...re angst...rest nag

Satan = Santa...as ant...tanas...sat? na...as tan...at san

Schoolmaster = the classroom

Scorpion King = Rock pig on sin

Sean Astin = sane saint

Sean Connery = on any screen

Sean Connery as James Bond = man, enjoy sacred, sane snob

Sean P. Diddy Combs = NY's cops did me bad

Sean Puff Daddy Combs = Duff CDs by a spade, mon...dances off, adds bumpy

Selena Gomez = sleaze gnome

Senator = treason…neo-Tsar…are snot

Senators = sane sort…assert 'NO'

Serena Williams = smiles, a real win…MAN-wise rallies…a Marseilles win…lean war missile…we smile, anal sir?

Miss Serena Williams = win slam, smile arises…I'm sassier, smell a win

Venus Williams = win slim values…win Slim's value

Venus and Serena Williams = US raven maids seen win all

The Famous Williams Sisters, Venus and Serena = won massive sums at tennis fields; share a rule

The Two Williams Sisters, Venus and Serena = wow, tennis rules lives and is mass theatre

Sex Pistols = sexist slop

Shakespeare = seek a phrase…he as speaker

Shakespeare, the Immortal Bard of Avon = Oh, this remarkable man's a favored poet

William Shakespeare = we ALL make 'is phrase…we all make his praise…I'll make a wise phrase…I am a weakish speller…he's like a lamp, I swear…I sleep-walk a ham, sire…a wee phrase? I am skill!

Shakira = I, a shark

Sharon Stone = no near shots…ass on throne

Sharon Tate = oh, neat star…threat as on…that reason…on a threats…sane throat…hate on star…heat on star…Satan to her

Sheena Easton = she's a neat one

Sherlock Holmes = heh, smells crook

Sherlock Holmes and Dr. Watson = handle damn, worthless crooks

Shirley MacLaine = silly maniac here…American yells: hi!

Shoeless Joe Jackson = cashless Jo's one joke

Sid Caesar = is a sacred…sacred as I…a crass die

Sidney Poitier = yet I do inspire…I desire no pity…is tidy pioneer

Sigourney Weaver = reviews anger you…revenge is our way…sure review agony…wieners voyeur, ag…view younger arse

Simon and Garfunkle = old man sang funkier

Simon Cowell = lemon, I scowl…I'm lone scowl…so lime clown

Simon LeBon = slime on nob

Sinead O'Conner = censored anion…no, in a censored…censor do inane

Sir Anthony Hopkins = oh no, his tiny pranks

Sir Francis Drake = I discern far arks…France's raids irk!

Sirhan Sirhan = harsh Iran sin…sin, harsh rain

Sir Martin Frobisher = for British mariners

Captain Martin Frobisher = batter Spain, horrific man…in a rampant British force…man force in a British trap…mariner chat: I ban profits

Sir Paul 'Bono' Hewson = oh so 'New Labour spin'

Sir Walter Raleigh = rather sillier wag…leer, sir? what a girl…girl has wart, I leer…is rather ill wager

Sir Walter Scott = writer's lost act…lo, writes tracts

Slobodan Milosevic = O, I'm an evil, cold boss

Milosevic = 'cos I'm evil

President Milosevic = is epic, devil monster...demonic, evil persist...I, devil, creep, sin most...I'm irritably omnipresent...blimey! I'm irritant person...MP's in a terrible minority...PM's in a terrible minority...bonny, premier militarist...I'm simplier, boney irritant...I'm born nasty, I merit peril...tiny merit or simple brain...simple-brain merit in Tory...I'm saintly, premier Briton...slimier rent-boy in armpit...mistily inebriant romper...IRA? liberty? imprisonment!

Milosevic vs. NATO = soon Slavic Vietman...involves atomics?

Smashing Pumpkins = I mash gimps 'n punks

Socialist = is stoical...O, class it

Sofia Coppola = asocial of pop

Soldier = dire loss

Son of Sam = of masons

Songwriters = worst singer...wiser, strong...worst signer...towers, grins...wore strings...worst resign

Sophia Loren = one posh liar...siren hoopla...O, no real hips...ha, poor lines

South American Indian = inhuman eradications...human in eradications...I not human radiances...I am an ethnic dinosaur...Draconian humanities

Spice Girls = pig slicers...crispi legs...Geri's clips

The Spice Girls = piglets' riches...crisis, get help!

Spiro Agnew = no rag wipes...gains power...worsen a pig...sowing rape...War Pigeons...a groin spew...wipe organs...grow a spine...grow a penis!

Spiro Theodore Agnew = here's no good wiretap...O, who? a

President Gore?

Vice President Agnew = deceptive answering

Stage Actor = got ace star…a great cost…O, great cast…O, acts great…get a co-star

Stalin = alt. sin…Latins…nilats

Stephen Hawking = he's the Pawn King…ps: he knew a thing?

Stephen William Hawking = when willing, I speak Math

Professor Stephen Hawking = he knew of proper ass things

Professor Stephen William Hawking = whispering phrases of Time, know-all?

Stephen William Hawking, the Theoretical Physicist = time/space was spherical. thinking? hey, to hell with it!

Stephen King = ps: ninth geek…thinks: pen, ge…get pink hens…*the King pens!*

Stephen King, Author = rank: he is the top gun…thank the genius pro…gent thinks up a hero…KO, pest haunting her…he repugnant shit, OK?

Stephen Spielberg = pig, best ever lens…best spleen giver…best PG, never lies?

Steve Allen = neat levels

Steve Irwin = interviews

Steve Irwin, the Crocodile Hunter = the television writher-conducer

Steve Martin = I'm star event

Stevie Wonder = er, doesn't view…strive on weed

Sting and the Police = spoil a decent thing…hot, clandestine pig…panic to this legend

Sting (Gordon Sumner), Andy Summers, and Stewart Copeland = Newcastle screen man: top plod, shy guitar nerd and some git on drums

Strip-Teaser = prettier ass…it's rare step…artist peers…artists peer…priest rates…it's star peer

Sugar Ray Leonard = rude salary, groan…your lad arranges…sure, a grand royal

Sugar Ray Robinson = brains, your groans

Suicide Bombers = bus, bodies, crime…ride bus, ice mobs…I describe so: bum

Sun-Yat-Sen = sunny East

Sylvester Stallone = slovenly steel star…over-talentless Sly…let's envy last roles…note Sly's star level…tarty, loveless lens…Sly l-loves teen star…totals nervelessly…relevant style loss…very less tall on set…only at stress level

Tea Leoni = O, an elite…O, alien ET…alien ETO…toe alien

Teddy Kennedy = dent dyke deny

Teddy Roosevelt = dolt-eyed voters…led destroy-vote…steely, odd voter…vote odder style…oddly steer vote…red-eyed TV tools

Televangelist = a gentlest evil…tells negative…evillest agent…vast, gentle lie

Templars = tramples

The Knights Templar = night, let them spark…kept things thermal…help that King's term…tight helmet pranks…met the slight prank…kept arms, then light…kept light, then arms…shh, kept mental grit…kept melting art, shh

Tennessee Williams = went senile as slime

Tennis Player = I earns plenty

Tennis Players = earnestly spin…sirens a plenty…Prannie styles

Terrorists = rotters, sir

The Allies = steel hail…e's ill hate…I, e's lethal…hill tease…see: hit all…a hell's tie…ha, let's lie…tie as hell…eh, last lie…tie a shell…a shell tie...the ill sea…I ate shell…elite lash

The All-Madden Team = damn medal athlete…madman led athlete…mad athlete in medal

The Amateur Thespians = inapt hams use theatre

The Amazing Randi = right and in amaze…mad haze training…hid amaze ranting…I am a grand zenith

The American Indian = I am in a thinned race…amid an inheritance…I am a ancient hinder…I am the nice and rain

The Americans = this mean race…main cheaters…main teachers…certain shame…maniacs there…men care a shit…he, cinema star…cinema haters…cinema arts, eh?

The Backstreet Boys = better sack the yobs

The Black Dahlia = Hail! Black Death…bill a hack death…hack, hate, ill, bad…the Kabala child…ha, ha, kill bad cat…ball a thickhead…ha, killed a cheat…a back hill death

The Bond Girls = born delights…bolder nights

The Boston Strangler = er, best 'n long throats

The Boston Strangler, the infamous Albert de Salvo = Mr. Felon gave blondes substantial sore throat…latest aberrant thing: marvelousness of blood…he's no blasted, arrogant, boastful, evil monster?

The Cantankerous Man = thus note a mean crank

The Carpenters = trash pretence

The Columbia Astronauts = acute human loss at orbit...brutal outcome hits NASA!

The Confirmed Bachelor = laced bitch? her for me? no...catch bold her? no, I'm free...femaled? chronic bother

The Coors: Andrea, Caroline, Sharon and Jim = CD's earn, Ireland has no hornier, major act

The Council of Nicea = ancient foul choice

The Dalai Lama = hell, I am a data...I, a, am all death

The Dali Lama = I am all death...I am all hated...I am tall head...hell, I'm a data...I a lethal, mad...halt, am ideal

The Detectives = detect thieves

The Doors = the odors...do others...so red hot!

The Duke of Wellington = O, fleet knight, won duel...one doleful, wet knight...fought on till weekend...would the King not flee?

Arthur Wellesley Wellington = well, well. English Tory nature

The Earl of Sandwich = he was often rich lad

The First Lady = has felt dirty...flirted hasty...shaft tiredly...flashy red tit

The Grateful Dead = death. fault: greed

The Grateful Dead, the American Psychedelic Group = dope-head trance music, duly get a real perfect high

Grateful Dead = dreadful gate

The Hiltons = hint: hotels…thin hotels

The Hilton Sisters = thirstiness hotel…shrineless, hot tit

The Human Race = earn much hate

The Israeli Army = her aims: reality…here's a military!

The Leading Man = I am the England…I'm elegant hand…I am gentle hand

The Married Man = I'm her darn mate…mated in harmer…trained hammer

The Married Woman = O dear me, in warmth…I'm no warmhearted…I am the warm drone…I am the modern war…I am the raw modern…I warm modern hate

The Moody Blues = embody the soul…the Loose Dumby

The Olsen Twins = new tits n' holes

The Osbournes = so bore us then…been sour, shot

The Other Woman = ahem, how rotten…a hot, new mother

The Pope and the Vatican = the avid, potent panache…pathetic and top heaven

The Prince of Darkness = he often snared pricks…had perfect sinners, OK?

The Queen of England = eh, end eloquent fang

The Republican National Committee = bump the total in American election…me patient? I machine-recount ballot…recount the ballot? I'm an emetic pain

The Rock = OK, retch

The Rolling Stones = hell, rotting noses…no one gets thrills…hell, sing so rotten…tell no singer's hot…seen, got no thrills…get no shrill notes…hello, snorting set…O hell, snorting set…lent one's hot girls…the Strolling Ones…greenish snot toll…is rotten hell song…sings rotten, hello…stolen Hitler song

The Rolling Stones Band = rant the bold songs line

Mick Jagger and the Rolling Stones = jerk dangles genital shortcoming…O God, talentless jerking. charming?

The Rolling Stones, Mick Jagger, Keith Richards, Charlie Watts and Ronnie Wood = heroic when hot, their Satanic Majesties wrinkled rock 'n roll, grandads to gig

Mick Jagger, Keith Richards, Charlie Watts, Bill Wyman and Ronnie Wood = Jerry Hall rid womanizer, wilting coke-head: rich twat, sad man, big conk

The Ageing Rolling Stones = heroes slogging in talent

Rolling Stones Band = real, not blind songs

The Ramones = the moaners…there moans

The Russian President = Putin hears dissenter

The Serial Killer = arrest, I like Hell

The Soldier of Fortune = to hustle friend or foe

The Soprano Singer = her top noises rang…phoniest groaners

The Star of Basketball = the fast, all-star Kobe B.

The Three Stooges = sheet so together…the hot ego resets…the ego tests hero

The Three Stooges: Moe, Curly and Larry = actors? Lord, they're an ugly threesome

The Trained Nurses = tender hearts in us

The World Rulers = lewd, lush terror…Order hurts well

Theodore Robert Bundy = note: terror-hobby, dude

Ted Bundy, the American Psychopath = happy hatred, unmatched obscenity

Theodore Roosevelt = heed, or lose to voter

Teddy Roosevelt = dolt eyed voters…odder style vote

Thomas Alva Edison = aha, ions made volts…anode has aim: volts…havin' amassed loot…vandal as smoothie…leads sham ovation…sham ovation deals…am evil, Satan's hood…a homo devil's Satan…avid asshole to man

Thomas Edison = a so, shit demon…I'm a sod, honest…I'm a sod, he's not…atoms do shine…I does no math…soon, math dies…ideas, not ohms…sat on his demo…do astonish me…notes aid ohms?

Thomas Gainsborough = hogs moot, brush again…aha, so go brushing, Tom

Thomas Jefferson = father of Ms. Jones…freemason shot TF…he majors, sent off…er, Tom has Jeff son

Thor Heyerdahl = hardly the hero

Tiger Woods = word: it's ego…ID: worst ego…wires to God…wire to gods…worst ego, Id do worst, git…got so weird…God, I towers…got so wired…writes good

Tilda Swinton = twit on island

Tim Burton = minor butt…mount Brit…I'm torn, but…I, Mr. Button…I'm burnt, to

Timothy Leary = I'm the royalty

Timothy Francis Leary = a tiny hysterical form

Tim Robbins = tin bomb, sir

Todd Rundgren = odd grunt nerd…drug 'n do trend…don't drug nerd…'d 'Runt' nerd, God

Tom Brady, Deflate = Mr. Lofty Deadbeat

Tom Cruise = I'm so cuter…Mr. So-Cutie…or Ms. Cutie…erotic sum…crimes out…Costumier…I'm cut, sore…I'm rose-cut…is more cut

Tom Edison = I sent doom

Tom Hanks = thanks, Mo

Tommy Lee Jones = molest me, enjoy

Tom Selleck = OK Stem Cell

Tom Wolfe = flow to me

Tony Blair = Tory in lab…lay Briton…try oil ban… by no trial…torn Libya…lay on Brit…bar it only…tiny Labor…a lib n' Tory…try on a lib…I, nobly rat…t-bony liar…I, ratly nob…lay 'bin' rat…liar by ton…Royal 'n bit…not by rail…I ably torn…try Albion…only a Brit boy, 'n trial…rainy blot…'n oily brat…orbit 'n lay

Tony Blair, PM = I'm Tory Plan B…boy 'n limp rat…my Briton pal…notably prim…yob 'n limp rat

Tony Blair, Prime Minister = men, I'm Britain's Tory peril

Tony Blair, the PM = trim, able python

Tony Blair, the Prime Minister = this Reptillian Tory Member in…I am bonny, prettier Hitlerism

Tony Blair, Premier = terribly minor ape

Travis Walton = now vital star

Trey Parker and Matt Stone = peaky retardants torment…top-rank, dreary statement…neater, rank, petty stardom

TS Caladan = at scandal

TS Eliot = toilets…is 'to let'…tits, ole

Thomas Stearns Eliot = hot tales, stories, man…a short name's toilet…so literate man hosts

Tyra Banks = snaky brat

Uma Thurman = unhurt mama

Unmarried Mothers = mourn their dreams

Uri Geller = re: guiller…ur, rig elle…I gel ruler…I, Ruler Gel…rule Eli, gr…r u leg riler?

Ursula K. Le Guin = sulk alien guru

Usain Bolt = sublation…sail but on…tail bus on…sunlit boa…I ban louts

Usain Bolt, the Sprinter = O pal best runner, it's hit…title is one sharp burst…sprain? burst to the line…it able in the run-sports…able in short petit runs…this stable, top runner…or I hit planet's best run…this bestial top runner…list I best top runner, ah…not in sharp-burst elite?

U Thant = that U.N.

Vampire LeStat = primeval taste…evil part mates…primaeval test…it vast empaler…primeval state…am vast reptile…part-time slave…sap time-travel…evil, apt monster

Vampirella = ample rival…a Marvel lip…evil arm pal

Vanilla Ice = ace villain

Vasco de Gama = CV, ma? a sea dog

Vegetarian = irate Vegan

Vice President = divinest creep…divine respect

Vice President Cheney = ripe, stenchy evidence

Victoria Secret Girls = over-critical tigress…is electric, star vigor…critical ego strivers

Victor Hugo = touch vigor

Victoria Azarenka = via Arizona racket

Victor-Marie Hugo = grim author voice

Vince Lombardi = brave, mild icon…verbal, dim icon…combined rival…manic lovebird

Virginia Wade = I ravaged, I win

Voltaire = I love art…la vie, rot

Waitress = a stew, sir?

Walt Disney = I lewd, nasty…I went sadly…it's new, lady…wildest? nay…Windy Tales…idlest yawn…wants yield…nits led way

Walter Disney = yields new art…drew in a style

Walter Elias Disney = we all desire sanity…yes, we installed air…yes, liar wants lies…really wise, instead…yes, I tell and I swear…wee silly Satan ride

Walter Cronkite = network recital…network article

Walter Koenig = low age in Trek

Walter Johnson = a low jet, non-HRs…no HRs, low jet? na

Walter Payton = to raw penalty

Warren Beatty = beware tyrant…watery banter

Waylon Smithers = swarthys oil men…wants him sorely…matronly wishes…many short wiles

Whitney Houston = Oh no, Whity tunes...O, nuts with honey...shut it now, honey...why shout in tone?

Willem Dafoe = low, idle fame...me, ideal wolf

William 'Bootsy' Collins = cool bass in lowly limit

William Clinton = an ill clown, I'm it...low 'n illicit man...low manic till in...I'm clot, all-in win!

William Jefferson Clinton = jilts nice woman, in for fall...female joins clown in flirt...fine: if in jam, controls well...jail Mrs. Clinton, felon wife...won small frolic in fine jet...firm, clean fellow, joint sin...major clowns, fell infinite...I'm well, confronts fine jail...finer joint, ill-fame clowns...fine, fine, still major clown...well, conform finest in jail...sniffle Cromwellian joint...fine roll, flown in Majestic...wolf, criminal, felon in jets...major felon in, in swift cell...clown joins finer fame, till...criminal-felons, flew joint...I'm well, frantic felon joins

President William Jefferson Clinton = we'll join Monica L. in stiff red present

William Clinton = lies? sin? little downturn? impeach!

William Clinton, the Former President of the of the USA = wiener fluid, hell, fat mother

President Clinton of the USA = to copulate, he finds interns...untense oral chief: don't spit...this fine nerd copulates ton...untested fornication helps...potent flasher in seduction...sod this intern of petulance...influenced honest patriots...if chosen, intern pulsated to...stated fool penis in her c**t...EU: Clinton spin Foster death

William Jefferson Clinton, President of the USA = finest neo-Fascist woman repelled junior filth...now posh sufficient jollier defamers in talent...intern fellated, major lies, now cut off his penis!

President William Clinton = lewd intent, sir. pill Monica...nice, limp, wild, total sinner...porn instinct? well, I'm ideal...mad politics, well in intern…well, it isn't manic, idle porn

President Clinton = content in red lips…'e split on D.C. intern…nondescript, let in

Bill Clinton = I'll nob in clit

Senator Clinton = nice? not! ran, lost

Ex-USA President, William Clinton = low cad: I must explain intern lies

Slick Willie Clinton = sick, not nice, ill will

Clinton and Bush = on bandit's lunch

Bill and Hillary Clinton = I call it horny 'n all blind…can rot in hillbilly land

William Faulkner = I'm an awful killer

William Hague = I'm a huge Walli…I mail huge law…I, I am huge wall…aw, I'm a huge ill…am lie, wail: 'ugh!'

William Randolph Hearst = amoral whilst philander…well-paid harlots in harm…sharp woman, ideal thrill…ha, ha, I'm ill-spent warlord

William Scott Bruford = drumroll of basic twit

William Shakespeare = I am a weakish speller…I'll make a wise phrase…hear me as I will speak…alas I'm shrew-like ape…wise male? ah, I sparkle…I make Lear's wish pale…I shape warlike males…I sleepwalk a ham, sire…a wee phrase? I am skill…we all make his praise…we like a psalm he airs…I swear I'll make heaps…weak lie? Lear's mishap…he, I, will make ass rape…I wipe hell's mask area…we shall make a pie, sir…we rape, kill a messiah…we are all ships I make…askew hell, I am praise…I am/was a killer sheep…I was here like a psalm…as a sharp, meek Willie…I am like a wheel rasps

William Shakespeare, the Bard of Avon = abrasive alpha male of the worst kind...he of silken phrase, at a live drama, bow...as I live and breathe, Mel's a heap of work

William Shakespeare, the Dramatist = was a peak, theatres still admire him...his art made him a star, we keep it all

Will Shakespeare = whereas I'll speak

Bard = drab

William Shatner = slim alien wrath...Will is Earthman...hair sit well, man...minstrel? ha, wail

William Tecumseh Sherman = meantime, chums, war is hell...we'll march in time, mesh USA

William Tunstall-Pedoe = teed up a Wall St. million...I do well plus I am talent...all unoptimised wallet...well insulated, optimal...well isolated platinum...a well-illuminated spot...I'd spell a mutation well...a lewd spell-mutation...ale limit pounds wallet...adult man is well polite...upset a man? I'll do it well...'la plume,' it isn't allowed... I'll slow up, I am talented...all input items allowed...still well-made utopian...Will's polite, adult name...O well, it isn't all made up...O well, isn't it all made up?

Willie Stargell = is large, well-lit

Willie Nelson = now ill, senile

Wilma Rudolph = do warm uphill...row mad uphill...do up warm hill

Wilt Chamberlain = recall: I'm with NBA...balance him, twirl

Winston Churchill = I'll crunch this now

Wolfgang Amadeus Mozart = a famous, German, waltz god...gorgeous waltz fan, madam...madman got far, Zeus aglow...warm gazes to a manful god...fur zealot gags madwoman

Women = won'em…own me…won me…me now!

Woody Allen = I lewd looney…wooed all NY…loyal owned…do one, Wally…wooden ally

Woody Guthrie = rowdy toughie

Wright Brothers = bright throwers

Wyatt Earp = a petty war

Yasser Arafat = a arse farts? ya…assayer at RAF…years as a fart…as a farty arse…ya, fare as star

Yasser Arafat, Nobelist = Arab, Israel often stays…a nasty beast for Israel

Yasser Mohammed Abed Ar'ouf Arafat = my dreams are of a famous Arab death…famed Arab's amateur army fades, Ooh

Yehudi Menuhin, Violinist = I divine one, shun humility…hi, I minuet in unholy dives…I'm in duo. I listen, huh? I envy

Yogi Berra = ye big roar

Zecharia Sitchin = hi, narcistic haze…aha, rich citizens…is rich, antic haze

Ziggy Stardust = zits, gutsy drag

Zoolander = razed loon

ANAGRAMACRON

The bizarre oddity of anagrams that tend to SPEAK also applies to the names of things, to words, phrases and titles of average, everyday objects all around us. Ever wonder WHY certain items, expressions, sayings, terms or organizations like 'United States of America' or 'The House of Representatives' or 'NASA' were named what they were named?

Anagrams give us an entirely new universe to explore and wonder about: *What a weird world we live in.* Is something from the Other Side or *out there* trying to communicate through anagrams? Coincidence surely occurs in a few cases. But repeatedly, again and again, jumbled letters display specific details that they should not know. Letters should not be *speaking* to us, informing us of occult secrets of what's beneath the surface of things...

And yet, very often, they tend to do so. Very often, they tend to be right. Why is that?

Anagrams of fictional things and fictional people also seem to 'speak' to us. Weird. Titles of books, TV shows or movies, when anagrammed, reveal the Magic. Is it in the air?

Is it white magic, black magic, alien or angelic communication or something else? Maybe it is an intelligence or consciousness we shouldn't fear? Maybe we should simply push the button of 'Anagram Genius' and enjoy the amazing knowledge/information given?

Remember: anagrams ought to make no sense. Why do they? What can we learn from them? The Anagramacron is far from a complete collection. Do your own research into odd anagrams. *You won't believe your eyes!* Anagram your name. What happened?

How was it that the ancients knew and venerated divine anagrams, while we modern people in the 'modern age' remain clueless? We're the ones with the anagram-generators. Or did the Egyptians and Incas and Greeks and Romans have better computers that we do?

AA Meeting = neat image

A Bacon, Lettuce and Tomato Sandwich = dad wants to eat a nice combo at lunch

Abbey Road Studios = obituary boss, dead

A Beautiful Mind = I am fine, but duel

A Black Hole = ah, able lock…a hello back…O hell, aback!

A Boner's Deep View = wide open beavers

Abortion Rights = is abhorring tot…go ration births…bin a torso, right?

A Bridge Too Far = RAF, brigade too

Absence Makes the Heart Grow Fonder = harshest teenager freedom now back...he's back, greater show of endearment...he wants back, dearest gone from here...and so be far to get smacker when here

A Candlelight Dinner = enchant idle darling

A Carton of Cigarettes = I got a taste for cancer…greatest of a narcotic!

Aces and Eights = assigned cheat

A Chevrolet = love the car

A Christmas Carol = art, Mr.? oh, a classic

A Christmas Carol by Charles Dickens = miser's character is coldly banks cash…miserly character bank cash. I scold…miser crank's cash charitably closed…shades scorn miser: call charity back…sans miserly character, so back child…hardback classic on arch-miser style…an old crass miser charitably checks…cranky boss cares: real cash, child Tim!

A Clockwork Orange = go, oral cock-wanker…OK, a real wrong cock…now look, crack rage…wacko Anglo rocker…Wagner cloak, crook…cool war-gore knack…kook crew go carnal…cage low rank crook

Across the Universe, the Beatles = Let It Be's verse echoes thru NASA

Actions Speak Louder Than Words = talk or airs cannot show up deeds…lips don't assure, can head to work

A Date Which Will Live in Infamy = if Machiavelli, deathly win, win…I am an evil child, if wealthy win…if Machiavelli, in wealthy wind

A Decimal Point = I'm a dot in place

Addiction = do acid, nit…I add tonic

A Dell Computer = a remote, dull PC

Dell Computers = result: model PC?

A Domesticated Animal = docile, as a man tamed it

Adult Novels = love and lust

A Farewell to Arms = realms of war tale

A Fashion Empire = is a phonier fame

Affectionate = oft a nice fate…to fat fiancée…eat affection?

Afghanistan = as in 'hang aft'…fan as hating…hang if Satan

Africa = far CIA

A Good Name is Better Than Great Riches = be not a hoarder, right acts gain esteem

A Hard Day's Night = ah, this grand day

Airport Security = criteria? rout spy…precarious? try it…priority act? sure...atrocity upriser...i.e. rout scary trip...is purer atrocity...pure atrocity, sir...ya, up terroristic...touristic prayer...rip touristy care...our epic artistry...true piracy riots...piracy is torture...it is corrupt year...sorry, I capture it...is to truer piracy

Alamogordo = O, good alarm...alarm God, Oo!

Alcoholics Anonymous = O my, no occasional lush

Alcoholism = mail school...so macho ill

Algebra = a garble

Alice in Wonderland = landed, won nice rail...alien and nice world...laced in inane world...nice inane world, lad...inane, new Caroll did...drew in on dalliance...irenical, new and old...wanna nice ol' riddle?

Alice's Adventures in Wonderland = verdant, nice lass due inane world...entrance, and inside world values...enslaved in unascertained world...educe verdant lass in inane world

Adventures of Alice in Wonderland = wanted: sneerful Leonardo da Vinci

Alice's Adventures in Wonderland, the Old Fairy Tale = a sure enchanter, ideal for Disneyland: Walt loved it!

Tim Burton's Film Alice in Wonderland = on Lewis Carroll, in mine but, daft mind...it's dominant, wonderful, bril cinema...brilliant cinema to wonderful minds...L. Carroll's on mine mind, but I fawned it

Alien = an lie...lie? na

Alien Being = I be in angel...in angel, I be

Alien Spacecraft = a scare, felt panic...faces panic later

All About Eve = love tableau

Allegories = lies galore

All Good Things Must Come to an End = glum note: good hedonism can't last...doing the last dance, gloom mounts...amusing the good-old malcontents

Allied Forces = oil-led farces...farce, oil lies

All Quiet on the Western Front = he'll question warfront tenet...the silent, eloquent warfront...lot on the frequent, silent war...rent this fat queen well, or not?

A Love Triangle = volatile anger

Alphabet = able path

Alphabetically = I play all the ABC

Alzheimers Disease = I realized he's a mess...aimless desire, haze...haze is real mess, die...I am desireless haze

A Magic Carpet Ride = impacted carriage

A Man and a Woman = a madwoman, Anna

A McDonald's Burger = real dog and crumbs

The McDonald's Restaurant = Dr.: a stunned stomach alert...such rotten...standard meal. McDonald's: the rat stue ran

McDonald's Restaurant = menu: rats and cold rats...mad c**t Ronald stares

MacDonald's = clam and sod

America = I'm a race...I, a cream...aim? care...I am care...I am acer...I am Race...a Crimea?

American = re: maniac...main care...rain came...main race...I care, man...in camera...are manic...me in a car...re: maniac...main race...I'm arcane...Cinerama...man, I race...in Mac era

American Bandstand = a mad cannabis trend

American Beauty = bare cutey mania

American Dream = aim? damn career

The American Dream = meet a dear, rich man

American Films = fame criminals…criminals' fame

American Football = ace ball formation

American Idol = demoniac liar

American Medical Association = I am an anti-social democracies…O dear me, I am a classic inaction…I am a concise, anti-social dream

America's Got Talent = a lot great acts in me…me on a 'great acts' list

America the Beautiful = I am beautiful cheater…I am the beautiful race…I'm a beautiful teacher…but a failure each time…amiable future, I cheat

A Middle East Arms Race = mad tale, dire massacre

A Mid Summer's Night Dream = is dad gum ham's merriment…damn me, Marish drugs time

Amityville Horror = I'm evil or harlotry

Ammonium Nitrate = a term, ammunition

Amsterdam = made trams…met dramas…mad master…dream mats…made smart…rest madam…mad maters

Anabolic Steroids = calibration dose…lab's idiots race, no?

Anagram Entity = *a tyrant enigma*

Anagram Genius = an amusing rage…gag in a surname…an

aging amuser…an enigma, sugar…amusing, a range…enraging Usama…amusing n' a rage…game runs again…gags ruin a name…a run: gems again…argue as naming…a sage manuring…amusing Reagan…name rugs, again…arguing seaman…a sure managing…a geranium sang…am a n**ger anus…name is Anu Garg…name is Garganu…suing a manager…using a manager…German iguanas…iguana mangers…ream aging anus…managing a ruse?

Anagram Genius, the Program = ah, upmost rearranging game…oh, get up, rearranging mamas

The Anagram Genius = huge, strange mania

Anagram Genius is Racist = great Russian magicians

Anagrammatisme = man, I am megastar…am a smart enigma…smart game mania

Anagram Mysticism = my magician's smart…swarmy, magic saint…I'm nasty, Mars magic

An Aisle = is a lane

An Alcoholic Beverage = gal, can I have cool beer?

Anal Retentive = a latrine event

Andromeda = Dear Nomad

A New Hope = a weapon, eh?

Angered = enraged

A Nightmare Scenario = Gore: an American shit…cheer Osama training…me snoring? I hear a cat

Animated Cartoon = cinema and art, too

Animated Movies = team made vision

Animated Motion Pictures = put cartoons in Media item…a pet in its cartoon medium…O, I print cat and mouse item…amused? I'm certain to point…used'm, I'm certain to a point

Anime Cartoons = some cannot air…is not a romance…I am not a censor…so, not American

Animosity = is no amity

A Nintendo Gameboy = made to be annoying

An Old Shoe = had no sole…on as holed

An Old-Time Christmas = St. Nicholas made trim

Antwerp = part new

A Pair of Patent Leather Shoes = there at a foot-apparel shines

Apartheid = a dirt heap…rapid heat…paid hater…a dire path…rapid hate

Apollo Landing Site = spot in Galileo land…I leap to Long Island

Apollo Thirteen = an or little hope…plot, or the alien…a trip to one hell…other alien plot…top latrine hole…not loathe peril…not literal hope…not halo reptile…not pilot healer…or patient 'hello'…to lonelier path

Appetite = pt: eat pie…ate pie, tp…PI: eat pet

Apple Computer Inc = complete up in crap…laptop PC? me, I run CE…I pun: complete crap…I turn PC people Mac

Apple Macintosh = laptop machines…am chips on plate…he's an optimal PC…compliant shape…is not cheap palm…heap complaints…ah, not a simple PC…top machine, pals…a simpleton PC, ha…PC: I am not a help…laptop PC? me, I run CE…I pun: complete crap…proclaim tuppence…Mac pulp core inept

Apple Records = deplores crap

A Promissory Note = payor remits soon

A Pyramid Scheme = ahem, spicy dream…is my cheap dream…pricey, mad shame

Arachnophobia = Oh, abhor, a panic!

Archeology = a glory echo

Arc of the Covenant = contract of Heaven…recent fan to havoc…cave, confront hate…for Heaven contact

Area Fifty-One = a fiery fate, no…eat of fine ray…on a fiery fate…fear a tiny foe!

A Remington Rifle = I'm long, neat firer

Are You Being Served = ignore/evade buyers…yes, rude verbiage on

Armageddon = do mad anger…and mad gore…am odd anger…goddamn era…darn mad ego…odd manager…drag a demon…dragon dame…made dragon…near mad god…among dread…are goddamn…Dear God, man!

Armed to the Teeth = demote the threat…deem to the threat…meet to the hatred…meet hotter death

Arms Race = Mars care

A Rolling Stone Gathers No Moss = stroller on go, amasses nothing…long grass on motionless Earth

Artificial Insemination = I fail? aim it in containers

A Sentence of Death = faces one at the end

A Set of Harness = fastens a horse

Asian Earthquake = a shaken, quit area…shak'n a quiet area

Asian Tsunami = sustain mania

A Signal of Distress = it's S.O.S. read in flags

Assisted Suicide = eased? I discuss it…aide discusses it…I cited sad issues

A State Reform School = home to foster rascal

A Stick of Chewing Gum = thing of magic we suck

A Stitch in Time Saves Nine = invest in machines, I state…since hem's in vain, I attest…this is meant as incentive?

Aston Martin = O, man transit

Astronomy = O my, no star

Astroturf = fur to star

A Suicide Note = tenacious die…in, cause to die…is cute idea, no?

A Tale of Two Cities by Charles Dickens = i.e. Darnay's cell switch, to see back of it…a head block is Carton's sweet felicity

A Telescope = to see place

A Tennis Match = static Henman…man, that's nice

Athens = as then

Athletic Supporter = the testicular prop

Atlantis = lit Satan…tin Atlas…it's natal

Atlas Shrugged = has ragged slut…Galt has surged

Atomic Bomb = BOOM at ICBM

Atomic Physics = I spy chic atoms…psychotic aims?

Attack of the Killer Tomatoes = freak title, a total shock to me

Attention Deficit Disorder = a stern doctor identified it

Australia = a trial USA…ultra-Asia…as a ritual…a urial sat…rail at USA

Australian Open = a super-national…a national purse…a star up? one Li Na…nasal epuration

The Australian Open = rule a top tennis, aha!

Austria = I USA rat…its aura

Avalon, Catalina = a vacation, Allen

Away in a Manger, No Crib for a Bed, the Little lord Jesus, Lay Down his Sweet Head = after a tired new mother's journey, a holy babe laid in swaddling clothes, awes

Axis Forces = scare, so fix

Baker Street Station = re: best trains to take…taste interest, bar OK?

Bally Total Fitness = silly battles on fat

Bargain Sale = an aisle grab

Baseball Opening Day = a playable nod begins

Batman Forever = a November fart…not braver fame

Battle of the Network Stars = fat or shortest wet blanket…not sweet-talk, fat brothers

Be All That You Can Be = obey, launch a battle

Beatlemania = I am a teen lab…I am an able ET…a beaten mail…am alien beat…I'm a late bane

Beauty and the Beast = shy, attenuated babe…haunted estate, baby…he sat by a debutante…ay, bet a stud beneath

Beauty Contest = bony, cute teats…cutey, not beast…eye to scan butt…not a best cutey?

Beavis and Butthead = thus, be a bad deviant…bad abuse in hated TV

Bedtime Story = most tired, bye…met tired boys…rest, embody it…body rest item

Beer Saloons = boosers' lane

Believe It or Not = I love to be inert

Benson and Hedges Cigarettes = best dog-ends, China teenagers

Berlin Wall = well bar nil

Big Brother = right b-bore…bright bore…birth, go reb

Bingo Game = ageing mob

Blind Faith = in bad filth…if bland hit…I, band filth

Boa Constrictor = I contort cobras…ribs contact, orr

Bohemian Grove = Romeo behaving…behavior on gem…boo, grim heaven

Bosnian War Crimes = Serbian racism won

Bottled Water = wet, bold treat…old, wetter tab

Brain Damage = grab a maiden…a mad bearing…I, a bad German…I, bad manager

Breasts = bra sets

Breast Implants = men's pal? bra/tits…meant bra splits

Bridget Jones' Diary = grand jeers by idiot

Britain = it, brain

Great Britain = battering IRA…giant rarebit…grit beat rain…grin, bare a tit…iterating: bar…I get a BR train

British Airways = this is war by air...is this wiry Arab?

British Broadcasting Corporation = horrid, patrician, bigot, snob actors...dictator Birt's phobic on-air groans...botching Birt's crap to air on radios...oh no, a boring Birt radiocast script...bigot chat radio: no script or brains...no, so irritating, drab, phobic actors...crap, irritating baboonish doctors...radio prohibits abstract crooning...snobbish, daring or patriotic actor

British House of Commons = fine, boorish, smooth scum

British Realm = her tribalism...bar Hitlerism?

The United Kingdom = O, dig the mud in Kent...I mightn't OK Dundee...I didn't go nuke them...O, it might end nuked...knighted? I'm not due...inn omitted keg, duh...guided men to think?

Budweiser = brew is due...I used brew...I brewed us...brew I'd use...weird us be...I sewer Bud...I dub 'sewer'...wired us be...I rubs weed...brew, us die...buried sew...is rude web...dew burles...wide rubes...U.S. bird wee...I brewed US

Budweiser Ale = wield USA beer

Budweiser, King of Beers = see foreign brew's UK's bid...so I befriend U.S. keg-brew...begs four risk, wee in bed

Budweiser, the King of Beers = I see huge drink, best of brew...drink best of brew, ghee I use

Budweiser Lager = bad, uglier sewer

Can of Budweiser = find USA beer, cow

Burning the Midnight Oil = 'high' until morning, I'd bet

Burying the Hatchet = hating the butchery

Butterfly = flutter by

California = racial info...facial iron...African oil

Calvin Klein Briefs = fine in black, silver

Calvin Klein Designer Jeans = cling near lad's knees in jive

Camelot = came lot…me lot CA…CA, to Mel…O, me talc…cat melo…camel to

Camelot, King Arthur's = our cream, last knight…ruler, knight, a mascot

Canoe = ocean

Capital Punishment = pain thumps a client…penal hit, amps cut in…times up, plainchant

Capitol Records = sold erotic crap

Carbon Dating = and boring act…on bad tracing…grant bad-icon

Car Insurance = races can ruin

Cartoons = no actors…no co-star…no scrota

Catholicism = comical shit…this comical

The Holy Roman Catholic Church = healthy, Catholic Church moron

Center Court = true concert

Center Stage = secret agent

Chariots of the Gods = horseshit! Act of God!

Charitableness = I can bless Earth

Charity Begins at Home = obeying Thatcher's aim…hatching Tories, maybe?

Chiapet = it cheap

Chicago Bulls = us: global chic…Club has logic

Chicken Noodle Soup = cooked luncheon sip...poison, choked Uncle

Chicken Soup = choice spunk

Chinese Fortune Cookies = I keen to censorious chef

Chinese Restaurant = nature has sent rice...taste ashen rice, run...nice anus shatterer...eat SARS in here...the rarest nuisance...the rats can run, I see...rats nuisance there...creatures hasten in...rice threatens anus...eat ethnic, arse runs...eastern rice haunts...Hunan retastes rice...Hunan caterer's site...eastern tuna riches...it's a sure enchanter...an ethnic treasure...authentic rareness

Chocolate Milkshake = smell the khaki cocoa

Christian = rich at sin...rich saint...INRI chats...I tans rich...rich is tan

Christian Fundamentalist = truth? fact is, man's in denial

Christianity = chastity, INRI...is tin charity...it's in charity...tiny, Irish cat

The Christian Church = ah, the rich, rich c**ts

Christmas = trims cash...its charms...charms sit

Christmas Eve = vicar's themes

Christmas Time = it emits charms?

Christmas tree = search, set, trim

Chrysler = sl. cherry

Chrysler Corporation = oh, cornerily sport car...oh, corner sportily car...pays lot, chronic error...lorry is crap, torch one...The Lorry Scrap Iron Co.

Church of England = changed for lunch

Church of Jesus Christ of Latter Day Saints = rich hot stuff castrates rancidly, oh Jesus!

Church of the Poisoned Mind = conduct homo friendship, eh?

Cincinnati Bengals = enticing cannibals

Cinematic Art = intricate cam

Circumstantial Evidence = can ruin detective's claim…can ruin a selected victim…instant crime, clue advice…a teen victim's crucial end…vet lacunae, indict crimes…even indict actual crimes…intact clue, saved in crime

Cirque de Soleil = is queer collide…idle queers coil

City of Los Angeles = gents say: cool life…easy, long life cost…fly, get casino, lose!

Cleanliness = all niceness

Cleopatra's Death = asp act, had to reel

Cleveland Browns = ever-bland clowns

Close Encounters of the Third Kind = cold feet or thin-skinned touchers…host children ride ten-cent UFOs, OK?

Clothespins = so let's pinch…to less pinch

Coca Cola = cool caca

Cocaine = ace icon

Coelacanth = a lone catch

Columbia = O, I'm a Club

Columbia Broadcasting Systems = busty orgasmic lesbian dom. acts…not sublime cosmic, bastard gays…immodest BBC analysts, gracious…a tidy combo: Uncle Sam's big stars

Coldplay, Paradise = 1.e. lads so play crap

Comatose = came to, so?

Commerce = CC, or me? me!

Commercials = cosmic realm…comic realms

Commit Suicide = is comic tedium

Committed Suicide = edit cosmic tedium

Communications Satellite = COMSAT: metallic, noise unit

Communist Manifesto = not immune to fascism

The Communist Party = icy truth, no PM's mate…traps the community…hyperactive, ant voters…is a pervert, convey that…vast, veteran hypocrite…nervy, apathetic voters…vet-craven hot-air types…can't revive Tory past, eh?

Compassionateness = stamps one as so nice?

Compensations = pass coin to men

Compound Interest = to do sum in percent…prudent economist

Computer = cute romp

Computers = O, spectrum…erupts.com

A Computer = our pet: Mac

Computer Virus = I've corrupt sum…corruptive sum…pure cur's vomit

Concentration = O, inner contact…connection, art…art connection

Conservative Party = prevents a voracity

The Conservative Party = teacher in vast poverty…reach vain, petty voters…paste the rev. vicar, Tony…O, teach perverts vanity…revive a snotty chapter…to vet vain Archer types…votes threaten privacy…re-activate NHS poverty…tap in the vast recovery...not very private cheats…stop Archer-vet naivety…hate prevents a victory…voracity prevents hate?

Conspiracy Theory = hysteric crap, no? oy

Continental Edison = clandestine notion

Contradiction = accord not in it

Conversation = voices rant on

Copenhagen = open change

Countries and Continents = unconnected transitions

Courtside Seats = so catered suits

Court Trials = curt to liars

Cracks a Safe = ask Scarface

Creationism = romanticize…is erotic, man…me, I cast-iron…I am corniest…ionic master…to nicer aims…merit as icon…I'm racist one…am nice riots…it is romance…it, one racism…iciest Roman…'e is romantic…it, I'm a censor…remain stoic…I'm so a cretin…reactionism…cinema riots…I am nice sort…action miser…it is ace norm…risen atomic…I'm so certain

Creator = reactor

Creature From the Black Lagoon = gloomful attacker abhorrence

Crime and Punishment = manic sinner thumped…chains imprudent men

Crime Does Not Pay = damper on society…comedy on pirates

Crotchless Panties = slot, penis catchers…horniest act less PC…spectacle in shorts

Cue Cards = accursed

Cure for Cancer = far occurrence

Customer Feedback = come, be daft, sucker

Customer Relations = to retail consumers…intercourse almost!

Customer Satisfaction = statistic of a consumer…focus: it is a rotten scam…infamous store tactics…famous in-store tactics…it is a fact to consumers…fast reaction is custom…fanaticism cost? so true…store's aim, contact us if…fairies contact us most

Daily News = idle yawns

Dallas Cowboys = colossal, bawdy

Dangerous = O dear, guns!

Darwinism = win mad sir…I mis-drawn…is mind war…is raw mind…I, mind wars…is raw 'n dim

Da Vinci Code = candid voice

Dawson's Creek = screw on a desk

DC Comics = cosmic CD

Dead Like Me = die, meek lad

Dead Sea Scrolls = local addresses

Dear John Letter = jet hated loner

Death = hated

Death Star = sad threat…Darth seat…stareth, da

Death Valley Desert = delayed the travels

Debit Card = bad credit

Declaration of Independence = no finer deed, an ideal

concept…fine peace intended, darn cool…it encoded pinnacle end of era…nice clip, denoted end of an era…end colonied era if act penned…I coordinate planned Defence…deprecate London in defiance

The Declaration of Independence = can pen a nice old deed of thirteen

U.S. Declaration of Independence = free land: nation seceded in coup

Signing Our Declaration of Independence of the United States of America = thirteen colonies post defiance dead against future foreign dominance

Deleted Scenes = needs selected

Delicatessen = ensliced eates…nice, dateless…cleanest side

Democratic Party = mad Tory practice…cite mad Tory crap…a mad, erotic crypt

The Democratic Party = ah, rated pretty comic…Mr. Cor, I detect apathy…try: dream hope tactic…pathetic try, Comrade…cheap dictator, try me…petty crime? O, act hard…I am the pretty accord

Democratic System = testy, cosmic dream

Department of Defense = daft feds rope teen men

Deposition = positioned…it, I snooped…idiot opens…I, deposit on…options die

Depression = person dies

Desiderata = dead satire

Desperation = a rope ends it

Destiny of the Human Race = if he's cute and horny, mate…face sin: hurt, money, death…the one randy fiesta chum…O, fun head test: machinery?

Detention = need it not

Determination = it remained not…not in time, dear

Detroit Pistons = ten sport idiots

Diamonds Are Forever = flavored, senior dream…vendor deaf or a miser?

Dictionary = indicatory

Diet = edit

Digital Camera = ideal magic art…die, magical art…dramatic, agile…I rated magical…I'm a tragic deal

Direct TV = credit TV

Disaffection = indicates off…in fact, dies of…fact of inside…defiant of sic…off Dianetics

Disease = see AIDS

Disneyland = end in sadly…deadly inns…dandy lines

Disneyland, the Happiest Place on Earth = I spent a day in her cheap hotel and slept

Disneyland Parks = kindly and sparse

The Disney Parks = hey kids, parents!

Disney Movies = in messy video

Walt Disney Pictures = we depict any lust, sir…nudity clips, we stare

Disney Television Channel = eye 'n listen, son. naïve child

The Disney Channel = see the child, nanny?

Disney World = old, dry swine…ends rowdily

Walt Disney's Magic Kingdom = it managed my scowling kids...claiming weak, stodgy minds...kid's own tidy, gleaming scam...calm kids wasting money, dig...admit mangey, scowling kids...I get mad, many scowling kids...giant ads welcoming my kids...and I wanted gimmicky gloss

The Walt Disney Company = want delicate symphony...what? not dynamic, Sleepy?

The Disney Corporation = O, porn enriches it today...hey, I noticed porno star

The Walt Disney Studios Animated Films = it is team style: Donald is made with fun

Disney Pixar = randy pixies

Distillation = do it in a still

Divorce Scandal = love can discard...dread volcanics

Dolphins = 'n old ship

Domestic Violence = see: condole victim...I'm conceited loves

Dormitory = dirty room

Dracula, by Bram Stoker = robustly dark, macabre...dark or subtle macabre...or Bela's murky, drab act

Dracula, Bram Stoker's Gothic Novel = cavalier monster tracks blood, ugh

Dracula, the Bram Stoker's Gothic Novel = lug-charmer attacks others' blood-vein

Drawback = backward

DreamWorks = mad workers

DreamWorks Animation = makers drawin' a motion

Dropping Acid = drip, God panic

Early to Bed Early to Rise = a rest or toil, bleary-eyed…bleary eyes or tired a lot…tolerable, yet I so dreary

Earth = heart…Terah…Thera…hater

Earth Day = Heart Day…death ray

East India Company = a spicey damnation

Eden = need

Election Results = lies, let's recount

Eleven Plus Two = twelve plus one

Emotional Insanity = a loony taint is in me…intimate as in loony

Empire State Building = I am entitled 'super big'

Endearment = tender name…mean, tender…tender amen

Engagement Ring = meet gangrening…gem 'n it, gangrene…tin gem gangrene…enter gang in gem…enraging gem net

England and France = fang and clean nerd

English Restaurant = hurts near genitals…internal gases hurt…lager has nutrients…natural green shits…stale herrings, tuna…sterling hares, tuna…hint: grease, salt, run!

Enterprise = serene trip

Erasure = use rear

Erectile Disfunction = concerned futilities…fertile nuts coincide…influenced eroticist…filter nice seduction…nice, fertile discount…often nicest ridicule…curse it, in, in cold feet…it confined cruelties…it lustier confidence

Erotic Massage = orgasmic tease

Esperanto = neat prose

Esquire Magazine = I'm a Queen-size rag…geez, risqué mania

Et Tu Brutus = u truest, but

Everybody Loves Raymond = loved by everyday morons

Every Cloud has a Silver Lining = via universally golden riches…hurray, all sin is gold even vice…irrelevancy is a lush gold vein

Excessive Drinking = sex, sickened virgin

Exodus = used ox

Experimentation = into extreme pain

Falling in Love = lo, an evil fling…filling a novel?

Fantasia, the Walt Disney Movie = his animated fantasy, we love it?

Fascism in America = I am a nicer fascism…I'm a man's sacrifice

Fear of Death = head for fate?

Fear of Flying = iffy for angel

Federal Bureau of Investigation = if found alive, abuse, interrogate…favorite agent buried alien's UFO…but a figure of evidential reason…O, for beautiful agents are divine…on average: beautiful, ironfisted…a beautiful giant is done forever…O, fine brutes favoured genitalia

The Federal Bureau of Investigation = nefarious, unadroit vegetable thief…agent adores favourite nubile thief…bat-eared, ultra-inoffensive toughie…hide a gun, steal it for a bit of revenue…a unit benefits a futile Edgar Hoover…taunt unit: disagreeable Hoover fief…a Teddy Roosevelt fief: a huge brain unit

The Federal Republic of Germany = for my gathered, peaceful Berlin…peace? bad energy from Hitler…ideal preference: fly to Hamburg…anger, fume by creep Adolf Hitler…peaceful by merger of their land…I fear a top French bully emerged…me be pure ally of French? I'd grate…a pedigree France? bully for them…I blame greedy French for a let-up…Pally at French border? gee, I fume…creep Adolf Hitler: my fear begun…life of large beer, much pedantry…can freedom-fight really be pure?

The Democratic Federal Republic of Germany = Adolf Hitler: genocide became my purer craft

Nazi Germany = I'm zany anger…aim: angry zen…gay men razin'

Feeling Romantic = flaming erection

Feminism = I'm fine Ms.

Field Goal = ideal golf…flag do lie

First National Bank = skinflint to Arabs

First Printing Press = fingerprints strips

Flattery = flat tyre

Flight Eight Hundred = eh, the filth drudging

Florida Gators = 'fro gladiators

Fluctuations of Stocks in Wall Street = a little luck wins, fortunes scoot fast

Flying Saucer = U.S. lying farce…fly using care

Flying Saucers = safely cursing…angel's sic fury

Flying Saucers and UFOs = Gray use fun disk, fan Sol…Grays use fun disc, lo fan…Large, fun discs, you fans…gods as funny as Lucifer…foul rays seducing fans…credulous fans in gay SF…classify dangerous fun…classy egos in fun fraud…feign classy fraud on us…O, large, funny USAF discs?

Another Flying Saucer = race of hunting slayer…searching nature, O fly…ain't UFO angry lechers…funnily, other gas race…UFO night races, nearly…any cue for Earthlings…eye for launching star…nuclear thing, foes' ray…years flouncing Earth…angrily confuse Earth…large, tinny, search UFO…launch, stay foreigner

Football = loft a lob

Football Season = notable as fools

Fornicate = fine actor…an erotic F…act 'on fire'

Fornication = in for action…a friction, no?

For Your Eyes Only = you siren foolery

Frankenstein's Monster = ten foreskin's remnants…note: transfer men's skin

Frankenstein, or the Modern Prometheus = representation of hunkered monster, hm

Frankenstein, Mary Shelley's = heresy yarn left man kinless…her entry yells: fake man, sins!

Mary Shelley's Frankenstein, or the Modern Prometheus = here, he reanimated smelly trunk of shy monster person

Frankenstein, the Bride of = abhorrent fiend's fit, keen

Freedom = fed more…me of Red?

French Cooking = chicken, no frog

French Cuisine = nice? chef ruins

French Foreign Legion = flog if nice greenhorn

French Restaurant = the France rats run…churn transfat 'ere

Fried Onions = in fine odors

Friendly Fire = rifle, fry 'n die

From Here To Eternity = theory of retirement

From Russia With Love = warm Soviet flourish…to film whore via USSR

Funeral = real fun

Galileo Galilei was Right = agilities haggle low liar

Garfield the Cat = de fat, lethargic…fat-care delight…Rat Delight Café

Garnet, Amethyst, Emerald = three neat art gems, my lad

General Accident = get a darn licence!

General Election = electoral engine…go re-elect a Lenin!

General Motors = or great lemons…go, real monster…loan, sort, merge…organ molester…a long term rose…angel restroom…a long term sore…strange Romeo…O, large monster

General Motors Corporation = lor, go monster car operation…lemon, or great scrap iron, too…O, O, earnings per motorcar, lot…more petrol or gas into car, no?

General Relativity = really integrative…elegant, arty, virile

General Theory of Relativity = I let ray of gravity enter hole…gravity too, referentially, eh?

Generation Gap = O, ageing parent

Geneva = avenge!

German Automotive Industry = anti-gravity, momentous rude

German Cuisine = menu is a cringe

Germany = my anger…grey man…Meg Ryan…angry? me?

Gibson Guitars = I, it, bugs organs

Gin and Tonic = dancing on it

Gin and Vermouth = hung over, damn it

Give Me That Old Time Religion = I am the loving God, elite merit

Global Warming = gag: I'm all brown…ball going warm

God Bless America = I massacred globe…slice 'em Arab dogs…I'd massacre globe…I'm a gross debacle…magic SOB leaders…obliged massacre…aged Rambo slices…bride's goals came…beg miracle, so sad…crises: geld Obama…big-car sales mode…a big dream's close…cars' bodies gleam…beg sacred oil, Sam…some big car deals…Sam's care obliged…gas, oil's embraced…declares: am so big!

God Save the Queen = quoted, he avenges…he'd avenge quotes

God's Message to Mankind = gets Saddam, OK, sign me on…man stinks, God made egos…OK, sign me, son. get Saddam!

God's Message to All Mankind = go to mass kneeling, add alms…seek glad monogamist's land…damn it all, seek songs, dogma

Gold and Silver = grand old evils

Gold Treasure = so ultra greed

Gone With the Wind = wow, the hit ending…gent went, how I hid

Goodbye Yellow Brick Road = lewd dayboy rock-idol bore…er, by book, gilded color way

Good News Miracle Bible Church = rich scholar mug: new Bible Code…chum who clings rare Bible Code…search own, rich, glum

Bible Code...Bible Code: high consumer crawl...war hero chum clings Bible Code...wiser Churchman log Bible Code...scholar grew much in Bible Code...church glamor is new Bible Code...son, Gabriel, which crumble Code...who clung richer Bible Code? Sam?

Goodyear Blimp = O my god, able rip

The Goodyear Blimp = get home by air? plod, I am the godly probe

Go Out With a Bang = a tough, giant bow

Gravity Waves = give wavy star

Great Depression = greater dopiness...pissed generator

Green Bay Packers = greenback payers

Greenhouse Effect = huge trees offence

Halley's Comet = shall yet come

Happy New Year = hype-weary nap

Hardwood Floors = hood of warlords

Harley Davidson = road-shy and vile...and is heavy, Lord...a sad, horny devil...shady and or evil...darn heavy, solid...hardy and so evil...old and heavy, sir

Harley Davidson Motorcycles = very costly old road machines

Harry Potter and the Chamber of Secrets = three chaps try to reach tomb, nerds fear...handsome heart-throb fear secret crypt

Harry Potter and the Goblet of Fire = portray battle of frightened hero

Harry Potter and the Half-Blood Prince = happy creator: enthrall, hot, forbidden...arch-fiend prattled honorable trophy

Harry Potter and the Order of the Phoenix = hide an extra depth of rotten horror-hype...tepid horror, poxy rot, then death. fan here!

Harry Potter and the Philosopher's Stone = horrid Snape threatens, hope, trophy lost

Harry Potter and the Sorcerer's Stone = horrors enchant stereotypes retard...treachery rests on transported hero

Harvard University = I try hard an' survive...Veritas: hard-run ivy...vends trivia, hurray

Have a Nice Day = have a cyanide...I've an ache day

Head Shop = hash, dope...shh, a dope

Heavy Rain = hire a Navy

Hell Hath No Fury Like a Woman Scorned = OK, unhealthy romance is her downfall...chained, folly, her man walks out on her

Here Comes the Bride = meet cherished bore

Heredity = third eye

Heroic Poems = O, Homer's epic

Heroin Addiction = aid her condition...her indication: OD...it hid an OD in core

Hibernates = the bear's in

High Times Magazine = might imagine hazes

Hip Replacement = the mean cripple

Hitler and the Swastika = star-like ant death-wish

Hitlerism = mirth lies...I'm slither...this Mr. Lie...let him, sir...Mr. Lie hits...slime hirt...is trim Hel...her limits

Hollywood = lowly hood...O, hollow road...oh, lowly do...do Holy Owl...how doll? oy...yo, who'll do...do holy low...doll why? O, O...yo, who doll?

Hollywood's Walk of Fame = Okay, well, model show-off

Holy Grail = girly halo...a holy girl...hail glory!

Holy Scriptures = story, such peril...priestly chorus...cruel sophistry

The Holy Scriptures = respect this hourly...ruthless hypocrite...true Christ helps, Oy...Oh, truths precisely?

The Scriptures = purest, richest...Christ's repute...he, true scripts...it hurts creeps...precise truths?

The Bible = blithe be

The Holy Bible = Oh, blithely be...I be by hot hell

The Holy Gospel = theology helps

The Holy Testament = let's note hate myth

Old Testament = most latent ed.

The New Testament = the new statement

Home-Based Business = he amuses 'boss in bed'

Home Box Office = Fox chief boo me

Homosexual Tendencies = exclude a she, so into men...unclean sex, he Sodomite...nude men, exotic a-hole

Honeymoon = money? oh, no!

Honolulu, Hawaii = oh, oh, wail in luau

Hors d'oeuvres = Oh, served sour...devour horses?

Horse Racing = ignore crash

Hospital Ward = low-paid trash

House of Lords = O, flesh odours...so rushed fool...O, rushed fools

House of the Rising Sun = eight-hour fun session...O sure, fine song, US hit...

ruin of gent, oh hussies...huge hit if on sourness...shut foreign sin house!

Houses of Parliament = shameful operations...home of spin? true, alas...loonies far up Thames...the amoral use of spin...loonies far up the Thames...home rates so painful...is a formal penthouse...a hateful spoonerism...Peel is a famous Rt. Hon....O, a thin forum pleases...O, i.e. neat splash of rum...loathe nefarious PMs...ain't a hopeless forum...Hoon: upstairs, female...I am poor hatefulness...house for pet animals...apes shout or inflame...meet piranhas so foul...aha, EU for simpletons...no faith slams Europe...a forum on the ale piss...phrase not famous lie...famous lies, torn heap...loon fart, misuse heap...pause on moral fetish...I'm a sheep fart, no soul...I am as the foul person...am hateful poisoners...as in foul atmosphere...eat foolish Superman...aura of simpletons, eh?

The Houses of Parliament = top man here's a foul shite...loonies far up the Thames...the shameful operations...the apes inflame or shout...often pushes lame hot air...see PM Hoon, that's failure...this foul ape moans there...them anuses fail poor...has lust on Empire of Hate...aha, stop the senile forum...a fearless Pitt, Hume, Hoon...forum: is not health asleep...the fat homo sapiens rule...the tearful homo sapiens...has elite human poofters...the foul or mean apeshits...the, uh, professional team...that's one heap of misrule...futile Hoon phrase, mate...PMs of a hostile nature, eh?

The Houses of Parliament, Westminster = their PM from No Ten, he is a useless twat...fear that imminent EU, powerless hosts

Parliament = rampant lie...I'm paternal...partial men...PM: a

Ten liar…armpit lane…er, napalm it!

The British Parliament = hint: the Imperial brats…hear prat Lembit in this…pan the Blairites mirth…that shit Premier in lab…BNP merits a hit: A. Hitler…I'm Blair, the threat: spin!

House That Ruth Built = that be shut-out I hurl

Houston,Tranquility Base Here, the Eagle has Landed = er, oh hi, hello again: ended a lunar quest by the States

Human Resources = secure man-hours…manure choruses…crush our enemas…run o'er such as me

Hurricane = churn aire

The Hurricanes = these churn air

Hurricanes Katrina and Rita = irk, raunchier, radiant Satan

I am the Greatest = the mega artiste

I am the Lord Thy God = odd girl at they home…ode: d'girl at thy home…Ed, do girl at thy home

I Can't Get No Satisfaction = 'cos a Stone can't fit in a git…a fantastic song, notice it

Id, Ego, Super-Ego = I, gorgeous deep

If at First You Don't Succeed = try deft, if cautious, second

I Feel Good = goofed lie

Ignorant = no rating

I Have a Large Penis = I please her vagina…he is plain, average

Illuminati = I am ill unit

Illuminata = I am all unit

I Love You Darling = you one valid girl

I Love God = good evil

I Love You = O, you live…O, vile you…O, evil you…Lou Voyie…you've oil?

I'm Loving It = omit living

Imagine = I, enigma

I'm Dreaming of a White Christmas = fading aim as thermometric wish…I'm sad from ice thaw, is nightmare…snow might reach far-sited Miami…with cameras, I made song firm hit…The air made this magic snow firm…harsh, firm, magic snow: I meditate…had frantic memoirs with images…I admit of: miss charming weather…is fearing mammoth thaw rids ice?

Impeach Clinton = let Monica pinch…point: cancel him…then, clip Monica

Impeachment = hmm, patience

Impossible = I'm possible

Impressionistic Art = artist's imprecision

In Alphabetical Order = airplane, boater, child

Income Taxes = exact monies…toxic enemas…examine cost

Incriminating Evidence = indicating a crime, even…indicate men in vice ring

Indecent Exposure = one's ruin expected…one sexed-up cretin

Indianapolis Colts = spinal dislocation

Indian Mascots = casinos, damn it…mad icon stains…amid sanctions…contain sadism…admission? can't. it is sad conman

Indian Restaurants = rat urine and stains…tuna is a dinner's art…art: nan industries

Industrial Light and Magic = magician hitting dullards

Industrial Revolution = loud roar, vile tinnitus…oil unto universal dirt…I turn around evil toils…villainous rotted ruin

The Industrial Revolution = untold virtue in earth's soil…untold evils to ruin the air…return a loud; oh, it isn't evil?

Inflammatory Bowel Disease = my ass blew fire, I moaned a lot

In God We Trust = twisted or gun…undergo twist…got weird nuts…it's wet ground…writes to dung

Innocence = once n' nice

Insanity = a tiny sin

Instant Replay = penalty strain…penalty in star…transient play

Insurance Company = manic Conner, pay us…I am uncanny corpse…no, a cynic Superman

Intelligence Quotient = quiet intent in college

Internal Revenue Service = receive a return, enlivens…a crueler sneer, inventive…I've earnt? seen clever ruin…eviler, reverent nuisance…relieve uncertain nerves?

International Business Machines = his ban is on ancient terminal's use

International Space Station = it is not a pleasant container…it is not a planet, or as ancient…O, CIA, antenna listens, patriot…scientist: talent? no, paranoia…nations ascertain potential…sail inane State contraption…plan is: rotate Asian continent

The International Space Station = I train that telescope on NASA tin…pathetic totalitarian nonsense…is planet Earth nations' action? ET…each teleportation is an instant…lone Captain's attention is Earth…threat? it's a pleasant: no nicotine…aliens'

attention, threat? so panic...ain't alone! interact on that, spies...Captain, it's a tenant's loo therein...toilet in a starship? not a canteen...attention, Captain, others: aliens!

Internet Anagram Server = isn't rearrangement rave...I, rearrangement servant

Internet Explorer = intent: expel error...next: net error pile

Internet Security Systems = scientists neuter mystery

Interrogation Techniques = CEO tenet: hurting no Iraqis

In the Bedroom = I'm hot-red bone

Invasion of the Body Snatchers = oh no, tidy heaven-born fascists...son of a bitch, thievery and sons

Is There Intelligent Life on Mars = those infirm little green aliens...little alien Engineers form this...tell the aliens' Foreign Minister...Engineers lift theatre millions...it's little green alien men or fish...literate green nets million fish

Is There Life on Mars = mires for the aliens...is a shelter for men, I...fret aliens home, sir...I hear monster flies...there remain fossil...this for mere aliens...no, shelter ramifies...alien mothers rifes...he site for minerals...other lifes remains...life remains, others...is aliens from there?

Italian Cooking = a coitional king...not a liking? ciao!

Italian Cuisine = I nail it in sauce...Sicilian auntie?

Italian Food = do in a fat, oil...oil and fat? oi!

It's a Wonderful Life = now strifeful ideal...now ill-fated furies

It's Been a Hard Day's Night = and hey, this band is great...British set, handy agenda

It's Beginning to Feel A lot Like Christmas = O big liar felt enchanting mistletoe kiss...tell Santa: come in, bring those gifts I like

Ivanhoe by Sir Walter Scott = a novel by a Scottish writer

Janet Jackson's Wardrobe Malfunction = breasts? now junk deft, canonical major...act on acute jam jar: fondles brown skin...narrow of obscene jackal: damn Justin T.

Jenny Craig's Weight Loss = joy, switching largeness

Jesus Christ was the Son of God = ah, we just do 'sign of the cross'...scorned Jesus was hit of Ghost...Christ now judges hosts of sea...God shows if the just Son cares...so God's son as Jew's chief-truth...If he saw just God Son, the cross...Jesus grows so hot, chief stand...so Jesus won fight, cross death?

Jets Win the Super Bowl = throw up in best jewels

Judgement Day = jet damned guy

Kentucky Fried Chicken = chef dick in turkey neck

Labour Party = Royal pub rat...abrupt Royal

The Labour Party = a prole? bury that...try our alphabet...upbeat harlotry...but, a real trophy...or abruptly hate...blather-up a Tory...ah, but proletary...a bluer, Tory path...beat-up harlotry...brutal, Tory heap

Labour Prime Minister = more spin? true, I'm Blair

Lactating Breasts = blast it, sag nectar...scatter a blasting...great cans, blast it

Land of the Free = fear often held

Large Breasts = great braless

Last Round of Drinks = fools isn't drunkard...lift on drunkard SOS...drunk of solid rants...if lost drunkard son...darn, drunk fool sits...unkind or draft loss...and drunk fool stirs...is not drunk for lads...drunkards lift soon

Last Tango in Paris = it is stag, anal porn

Las Vegas = gas slave…salvages

Las Vegas, Nevada = savage, venal, sad

LA Times = it's lame

Lawrence of Arabia, the Film = noble, white male, far Africa

Laxative = exit lava

Leonardo Da Vinci's The Last Supper = depict all persons and the Saviour…ends: avid apostles repair to lunch…Opus Dei Dan: Christ veal on plaster…apostolic pleasure: had TV dinners…converted us, appalled historians…Leo, on this dried-up plaster canvas…an arch-devil's on Opus Dei platters…hundred live snails, carp potatoes…ensure lad's liver and potato chips…Italian spuds preserved on a cloth…painter hands apostle crud olives…overdone lunch, I tasted appals, sir…Christ devoured snails on plate, Pa…our CV's apostles heralded in paint…do paint us sloven pilchard eaters…vast colour he's a splendid painter…Opus Dei: Christ, darn veal on plates…*Vicar Tunstall-Pedoe praised nosh*

Leonardo Da Vinci's Drawing, The Last Supper = I arrange twelve pupils and soon add Christ

Les Folies Bergere = rosier, feeble legs…or feeble legs rise

Le Tour de France = race round fleet

Levi Jeans = able juveniles

Life After Death = I'd feel that fear…I fade, left Earth…felt dire fate, ah…fate, it held fear…ah, fate filtered…halt! I defer fate

There's Life After Death = freed as I left the Earth

The Afterlife = felt fire, heat…let faith free…I felt her faith…I felt the fear…I left the fear…feel that fire!

Life Insurance = finer lunacies…a fine, cruel sin…insane Lucifer…finance is lure…is funeral nice?

Life, Liberty and the Pursuit of Happiness = this friendly, beautiful, happiest person…up filthy President, if he plots Iran abuse…land of suit-happy, purse-thief libertines…O, find the reliable path: fruit, pussy, penis!

Life on Mars = alien forms…so frail men…from aliens…if man's role…flame or sin…film reason…men of liars…iron flames…farm on lies…Roman files…of minerals…no slim fear…moral fines

Life's Aim = families…families?

Like a Virgin = I like raving

Listen = silent

Listened = enlisted

Little, Red Riding Hood = girl idol, thirteen odd

Live Aid = evil air…avid lie

Live and Let Die = invalid? delete

Lobster Fisherman = harms fine lobster

Lock, Stock and Two Smoking Barrels = slow, lacking darkness, rock bottom…do let's clock Sting's barman work, OK?

London Bridge = old or bending

London, Great Britain = land of Breton origin

Look Before You Leap = O, peek, or you'll be oaf

Lord of the Rings = God's thorn rifle…Frodo, shire, LTNG…stronghold fire

Lord of the Rings Trilogy = good, fiery strong thrill…Oh, godly, stifling terror

The Lord of the Rings Trilogy = horny egos fight, tired troll

The Lord of the Rings = he'd long for her tits...third of long threes...Frodo's nether light...night shelter Frodo...shelter thing, Frodo...trod length of Shire...strong elf hit horde...front the Shire gold...errs on the old fight...elf got red rhino sh*t...the filth errs on God...the filth errs, no God?

The Lord of the Rings by Tolkien = hot, trendy, filling three books!

The Lord of the Rings by John Ronald Reuel Tolkien = thrilling nether-land journey of three old books

JRR Tolkien's Lord of the Rings Trilogy = torrid, gory, elf trek: thrills, join song!

JRR Tolkien's The Lord of the Rings, the Fellowship pf the Ring, Volume One = help join trek West then South of Shire length. Frodo fell in River Gloom

The Lord of the Rings, the Two Towers = Frodo, the gentlest whore's is worth it

Lord of the Rings, the Return of the King = hero-like truth or offending strength...frightened knights honour elf torture?

Lord of the Rings, Return of King = Frodo's keen, hunting, terror-flight

JRR Tolkien's The Hobbit or There and Back Again = hear, hear Bilbo at Bag-End! join hot tricks 'n trek

Los Angeles = sells an ego...Angels lose...sells and ego...all's seen, go

Los Angeles Angels = gal ogles leanness

Los Angeles, California = so if all clean air's gone...no angels, local fairies…casinos legal? no fear…gasoline: one fills a car…galleria confessional

Los Angeles Clippers = Los Angeles Cripples…collapsing? peerless!

Los Angeles Lakers = sells oranges, kale

The Los Angeles Lakers = sneakers sell the goal

Los Angeles Police Department = dragnet people toss me in a cell…crime agents: all stoned people

Los Angeles Times = glee, Ms. it's on sale…logs tense emails

Love at First Sight = flash tits, vertigo…so that flirts give…this fat girls vote…love is fast, right?

Love is Blind = blond is evil

Low Fat Food = flat, of wood

Lubrications = oil acts in rub

Lucy in the Sky With Diamonds = ho-hum, tiny, tiddly wackiness…hey, win shoddily sick mutant…nasty, wonky, childish tedium…sunny, witchlike sham oddity…yum, a kindly hedonists' witch

Lysergic Acid Diethylamide = giddy, chemicalised reality

Mad Cow Disease = a sad cow demise…doc saw a demise…ID meadow cases…a wisdom ceased

Madison Square Garden = odd anagrams enquires

Magna Carta = anagram act

Make Fun Anagrams = manage fun karmas…manage 'nuf karmas

Make it so, Number One = beam me neutrinos, OK?

Male Chauvinism = valium machines…I'm such a vile man…ah, I'm an evil scum…ah, masculine vim

Males Never Ask for Directions = keen crisis of men's road travel

Malibu Beach = amicable hub

Manchester United = the nut's named Eric…this decent manure…ruined tense match…untested chairmen…Red men? I hate c**ts…entertained chums…dents a Munich tree…the unarmed insect…MU, the ancient reds…cretins and the emu…rent Dutchmen, I see…the nice name's 'turd'…ten in red, such a team…MU: ten cheats in red…the dire, mean c**ts…rich, mean, untested…untethered maniacs…nutters can hide me…The Entrained Scum…Munich ate ten reds…cremated nun shite…stained hen rectum…urine detachments…the innate red scum…nice team thunders…riches taunted men…'n I hate 'em red c**ts…me, I chant Red tunes…red menace: hit nuts…red teens at Munich…Dutchmen trainees…shite name, red c**ts…her c**t's dementia…entrenched autism

Manchester UTD = the dream c**ts…the red sanctum

Manic Depression = ends in 'I'm a corpse'…panic demons rise…prime dissonance…snip, romance dies

Manifest Destiny = finest dynamites

Many a True Word is Spoken in Jest = men joke and so win trusty praise

Marihuana = a human air

Marijuana Deal = a man, a rude jail…man-jailed aura

Mark of the Vampire = freak VIP to Hammer

Marlboro = rob moral…molar rob

Marriage = a grim era

Married = admirer…dire ram…ram ride

Married Life = life admirer

Mars = arms!

Marseilles = real slimes

Martin Luther King Day = thinking: truly a dream…maligned Ray hit trunk…guilt? think 'n armed Ray

Marvel Comics = comic marvels…cosmic marvel…Mr. Comic Slave

Mashed Potatoes = smoothed, as pate

Masterpiece = see crap item…escape merit

Masturbation = it's nob trauma…anatomist rub…a moan, it burst…aunt omits bra…O ta, man rubs it…bust animator…rub at it, moans…Maria's button…rub tits, a moan

McCarthy Era = my character…my rare catch

McCarthyism = mystic charm…cry mismatch…Mr. Scary Itch…cram sic myth…hmm, scarcity

Measured = made sure

Measurements = man uses meter…numerate mess

Medal of Honor = damn fool hero…of modern halo…hero of old man

Medicinal Marijuana = a cure? I'm in a damn jail!

Mein Kampf = am pink fem

Mein Kumph = hmm, in puke

Mein Kampf by Adolf Hitler = my platform: kin had belief…OK, print my half-mad belief…bimonthly piffle, Kamerad…imply it baffled Herman, OK?

Melodrama = alarm mode

Membership = hmm, sip beer

Menage a Trois = an orgies team…game senorita…sane trio game…eaten, I orgasm…ignores a mate…Tories manage…organize team

Men From Mars = Mr. Mean forms…arms form men

Menstrual Cramps = spasm, return calm

Mercury, Venus, the Earth, Mars, Jupiter, Saturn, Uranus, Neptune and Pluto = just nine planets may arc up round the Sun, ah, pure art ever true must run…just vacuum, nine planets turn around Sun: her rays put her temperature…my, just vacuum. her part: nine planets turn around Sun, true super-heater

Merry Christmas = crass myrrh time…martyr smirches…rich martyr mess

Merry Christmas and Happy New Year = starry hype many wrap merchandise

Message in a Bottle = items belong at sea…able seaman's got it

Metaphysical = mystical heap…empathics lay…typical shame

Meteor = remote

Metronome = toner memo…Moon meter

Miami = I maim

Miami Heat = I am the aim

Mickey Mouse = eek, music! Oh, my…yo, meek music…key: U.S. commie…OK, use my mice

Mickey and Minnie Mouse = mean, kid mice: money in U.S.

Microsoft = is comfort…stoic form

Microsoft Corporation = moronic sort of apricot

Microsoft Windows = I'd wow conformists…MSDOS friction, wow…moron disc fits, wow…wow, so I'm first on CD…fits in CD-ROM, so wow…wisdom, or swift con?

Microsoft Windows XP = worm downs PC, so fix it…fix worst, dim PC OS now!

The Microsoft Corporation = motto: 'rich fornicates poor'…to protect horrific OS? O, man…torch fair competitor soon…horror of competition acts

Microwave = warm voice

Microwave Oven = O man, revive cow…cow revive, moan

Middle Earth = mild-hearted

Military Actions = it's amoral in city…calamity, riot, sin

Military Headquarters = red alert: U.S. may hit Iraq

Military Service = scary, virile time…it carries my evil…my evil, it's racier…i.e. rarely victims

Milton Bradley = old man Liberty

Miracle = reclaim

A True Miracle = material cure…I am a lecturer

Miracle Hot Springs = got clean shrinp, sir?

Miracle of Fatima = I'm factorial fame

Miranda Rights = it is grand harm…I'm daring trash

Missing Persons = Spring Session M…impress in songs…impressing sons…sings on, impress

Mitsubishi = I, I'm this bus

Mitsubishi Corporation = I prohibit crimson autos

Modern Times = dire moments

Mona Lisa = a man's oil…I'm so anal…Ali Osman…an oil, a ms.

The Mona Lisa = ah, not a smile?

Da Vinci's Mona Lisa = maid in oils, canvas

Leonardo Da Vinci's the Mona Lisa = Oh, her odd, Italian smile on canvas

The Mona Lisa Gherardini Del Gioconda = hanging art, I smile. Leonardo hid a code

Mondays = dynamos

Money = my one…mo yen

Monty Python's Flying Circus = strongly psychotic, I'm funny…mostly funny, chronic pigsty

Mother Nature = humane rotter…the Numerator

Mother of Mercy = my, eh, Comforter?

Mount Saint Helens = as eminent hot nuls

Mount Rushmore = must mourn hero…mushroom tuner

Mouth-to-Mouth Respiration = honour throatiest optimum

Mr. Potato Head = harmed potato

Munich = I munch…much in

Music Television = sit, volume is nice…I'm voiceless unit…it is nice volumes…elite, scum vision

Music Videos = I, us move disc…is voiced sum…I move

discus…I've sum disco…us, dim voices is scum video

My Name is Bond, James Bond = enjoys madmen and bimbos…man enjoys damned bimbos…snob jammed by insane mod…bonny names, mad Jedi mobs…same bed, son: mind my banjo

Mystery Tour = my true story

My Sweet Lord by the Former Beatle George Harrison = GH regrettably a 'He's So Fine' melody/meter borrower

My Television = misty, evil one…it's evil money…tiny movie sel…I'm violent, yes?

NASA Releases New Stunning Images of Mars = signal saw green men ass, see far mountains

NASA Space Program = rampages on as crap…maps sap arrogance

NASA's the Curiosity Rover = aha, I try to cross universe…ah, necessary tour visitor

The Mars Rover Curiosity = my tour visit or research?

The Rover Curiosity = very historic route…very heroic tourist…its very hot courier…is our victory there?

NASA Video Shows Ancient Mars as Lush, Water World = wet nature, lavish swims, Lord: now area's sand, chaos

National Aeronautics and Space Administration = aim is to land pods in/near USA area. can it? no, it can't

National Geographic = gaining a clear photo…on giant archipelago…O Anthropical ageing…help coronating Gaia

National Hockey League = a leak on ice? Ole, naughty…huge Yankee allocation

genuine coke Ayatollah…note huge alliance, okay?

National Rifle Association = of anti-social or an alienist…is fool, anti-social, inane rat…I an anti-social, nastier fool…fool in an anti-social satire…strain of social alienation

National Security Agency = tail, to enrage any U.S. cynic

Natural Selection = alter ancient soul…ancestral outline…it's no nuclear tale…clean out latrines…rule, *attain clones*

Neon Lights = not English

Nepotism = I'm pet son

Neverland, Michael Jackson = major nick and cell, heavens!

New Labour Party = a true Brown play…Brown up later, ya…a blue Tory prawn…Brutal weaponry…war! pan blue Tory…Brown at rule, pay!

New Order = now erred

New Orleans Saints = Satan winners lose…nonessential wars…sensational wrens

Newspaper = pans repew…reap 'n spew

New York = worn key

New York City = yet, Rocky win

New York Times = monkeys write…emits wonkery…skew enormity

The New York Times = I wrote keen myths…monkey wits there…monkey twits here…key men wrote this…they strike women…hit key metro news…tree with monkeys…wonky items there…worthiest key men…I knew story-theme…the wet, inky Morse…seek written, oh my…the monkeys write…write keen mythos…esteem worthy ink…wee mythos tinker…we key mirth notes…we ink story theme…three times wonky…he knew story item…wrote inky themes…thy Semite knower…New York, meet shit…key the wit sermon…History went meek…I key hot news term…enmity worksheet…hey, written smoke…Yonker's wit theme…wet, inky theorems…town's key merit, eh?

New York Transit Strike = Yonker's wit: trains? trek!

New York Yankees = key: sneaky owner

Niagara Falls = rainfall saga

Nightmare on Elm Street = the norm, grim, tense tale…relating monster theme

No Admittance = contaminated

Nominate = a mention

Nonsense = seen 'n son…Ness? none…seen 'n nos.

North America = richer, to a man…roam in the car…one matriarch…macho terrain…in macro earth…I am the rancor…Monica? rather…ah, incomer art…I'm rather a con

North Atlantic Treaty Organisation = rational anger, shoot Titanic tyrant

Norton Antivirus = innovators run it…turn vision on art…it runs innovator…not torn in a virus…I turn innovators…I via runs, torn not…run its innovator…no, not train virus…Sir Innovator Nut

Nova Scotia and Prince Edward Island = two Canadian Provinces, lands I dread

Nuclear Blast = brutal cleans…as clean blurt…brutal lances

Nuclear Fallout = foul ultra clean…a cultural felon…call foul nature…ace of ultra-null

Nuclear Physics = unclear physics…neural psychics

Nuclear Power = new, purer coal?

Nuclear Power Station = a near core, lit-up towns...raw, utopian electrons...it also current weapon...one certain plus to war...option's true, clean war...in a plot: new U-reactors

Nuclear Reactor = an ulcer creator...run accelerator...run coal retrace

Nuclear Weapons = cleans up one war...war plan: use once...as unclean power...now a secure plan...clean up one's war...learns a new coup...plan a new course...an answer: couple?

Nutrisystem = yes, trim nuts...is nuts, try me...ye trim stuns...is my test-run

Oakland Raiders = so irked rad anal...adored Sri Lanka...naked railroads

Octopussy = spy cuts, Oo!

O.J. Simpson Trial = spoilt major sin...romp to jail sins...jail moron spits...jail, sits on romp...so split in major...icons jam spirit...I no major splits...most jail prison...posts minor jail...I'm jail, on sports...minor jail stops...is top, jail norms...pilot major sins...pilots major sin...is torn jail mops...I major spin, lots...jail romps, is not...I'm no jail sports...Sports: I'm no jail...moron's jail tips...I'm no jail romps...spoils joint ram...is not major slip

O. J. Trial = jail rot

The O. J. Trial = hotter jail...the jail rot...jet hot liar

O Little Town of Bethlehem = no hotel to befit them well

Oliver Twist = I've writ lots...twit is lover

Oliver Twist by Charles Dickens = wretched Victorian's Bill Sykes...swarthier Bill Sykes convicted...'not wicked' Bill's crass thievery...wicked clever boys instil trash...I've child's best work, it's larceny...very twistable kids' chronicles...a very wit-blessed kids' chronicles...wiser driven to catch Bill Sykes...lost kids: terrible, chancy views...catch Bill Sykes, town: Riverside...the direr convict was Bill Sykes...

Oliver Twist, the Novel by Charles Dickens = scrawny bloke sent child to thieve silver

Olympic Games = employs magic...gimme Calypso

The Olympic Games = each pommy legs it...mighty males cope...mighty leaps come...it's pommy leg-ache...thy images compel...my gospel, I'm cheat...someplace mighty...my cheap log times...O my, glimpse cheat

Once Upon a Time = continue a poem

One Dollar = older loan

One Good Turn Deserves Another = no, roques never do endorse that...or need, soon avenge stored hurt?

One Night Stand = snog, and then 'it'

One's Birthday Suit = this nudity so bare

Onward Christian Soldiers = Lord is at war, sends in choir

Orbiting the Moon = one bright motion

Orbiting the Sun = burning-hot site

Orbiting Venus = observing unit

Our Marvelous Planet Earth = pure love, as natural Mother...a supernatural Love Mother...home, love, natural raptures...a manor: truth, love, pleasure...a love or man-pleasure truth...rapturous, maternal love, eh?

Oxford University = fury, no sex, VD? I riot...forty Durex vision...ivory fixtures, Don

Paint Your Wagon = gun-wary, I pan too

Palestine = penalties...alien pest

Palestine Liberation Organisation = I go plot a riot in Israel, an insane bet

Palestine Liberation Organization = Israel at a TNT blaze, I ignore opinion

Palindromes = I'm a splendor

Palomar Observatory = lo, a starry romp above

Paradise Lost = despairs a lot…a pal dies, rots

Paris = is par…pairs

Paris, France = I reap francs…fear crap, sin

Parkinson's Disease = so rapid sneakiness

Parsons Green Station = seen trains stop, groan…inane egos transport…so-arrogant ineptness

Patriot Interceptor Missiles = timeless airstrip protection

Payment Received = me paid every cent

Peace on Earth = race hate? nope…repeat an echo

Pendulous Breasts = topless, bra unused

Penthouse Magazine = a pouting semen haze…amaze not huge penis…humane pet agonizes…seize, moan, huge pant…ahem, stage one: unzip…oh, gauze panties, men…O, men gaze at nips' hue

Pentium Processor = computerises porn…O, sportier men's CPU…prisoner computers…opens computer, sir…CPU, more porn sites

Pepsi Cola = a pop slice…pop a Slice

Pepsi or Coke = spook recipe

Permutation = utopian term

Pinball Machine = nimble chaplain

Pink Floyd = dinky flop?

Pittance = a cent tip

Pittsburgh Steelers = better ruthless pigs…best repulser tights

Pixar Films = fix lamp, sir

Pixar Animation Studios = I am spirituous and a toxin…utopians Marxian idiots

Planet Earth = eternal path…penal threat…plant heater…late panther…heal pattern…the plant era

Planet Earth from Space = see, pen flat chart or map

Planet Earth, Our Marvelous = pure love as natural Mother…home, love, natural raptures…a manor, truth, love, pleasure…truth, love or a Man-pleasure…rapturous, maternal love, eh?

The Planet Earth = elephant threat…the eternal path

The Earth = the Heart

Planet Hollywood Restaurants = loud 'Lethal Weapon' stars try-on…Woody Allen on plates hurt star…taste another lousy prawn, doll…a pretty Sharon Stone, all would…spot Woody Allen's the LA rat-run…spot the rotundly arse on LA Law…Houston and Walt poster? really…Tunstall-Pedoe's Norway harlot…on LA Law part: untold oysters, eh?

Plan Nine from Outer Space = run poorest film, a penance…one man's picture near flop

Please Hold the Line = telephone aids hell

Pluto = u plot…lo "T" up…lot up…to pul

Pluto is a Planet = appeal to insult

Planet Pluto = a potent pull

Poems are Made by Fools Like Me But Only God Can Make a Tree = no Blake, somebody Kilmer may generate so famed a couplet

Poetry = try Poe

Poison = in, oops!

Poker Game = romp a geek

Police = cop lie…I, le cop…I, el cop

Police Department = talented prime cop

Police Raid = periodical

Police Station = I listen to a cop

Polly Wants a Cracker = sly parrot, cackle: naw

Poltergeist = let go, sprite

Popularity = up polarity

Pornography = horny rag, pop

Positively No Admittance = no place to visit any d' time

Precaution = I put on care

Precipitation = tip: poetic rain

Predestination = oriented in past

Predomination = I'd remain on top…monitored pain…top Iron Maiden…Mr. Opinionated…not so impaired

Prenatal = parental

Prenuptial Agreement = get meaner near pulpit

Presbyterian = best in prayer...bent, pray, rise...priest nearby...beer party? sin!

Preseason Football = bores pleasant fool

Prestidigitation = presto! a digit in it

Prince of Tides = ps: I cried often

Princeton = not nice PR

Produce = crop due

Professional = pain of losers

Professional Wrestling = O, lifts large person: wins...inspires a strong fellow...new girl in less of a sport...is sport of, well, earnings...foil largest person's win...lines grow in false sport

Prostitution = in/out, sport...to put into sir...pro tits, in, out

Psychedelia = LSD epic, yeah

Public Relations = crap, built on lies...sprout brilliance...social blueprint...prosaic bulletin... so put, brilliance...Republicans toil...I practise bull, no?

Quantum Theory = query: atom hunt?

Queen and Country = any conquered nut

King and Country = tyrannic dung OK

Rachel Ray Show = oh, a cherry slaw...rarely has chow...her scholar way

Radio = do air

Rage Against the Machine = I hate the American gangs...*he gets a hit, nice anagram!*

Raiders of the Lost Ark = Ford, the real star is OK

Rap Music = up racism

Rational = not a liar

Reactor = Creator

Reader's Digest = registered ads

Read the Script = decrepit trash…tired chapters

Reality Shows = this year's low

Real Madrid = admire lard

Real Time With Bill Maher = I'm the warm liable Hitler…I'm the liberal warmth lie

Red Light District = third leg district

Red Light Districts in Amsterdam = Mr. 'Smith' and distracted girl

Red Lights in Amsterdam = stranded girl mates him

A Red Light District = it adds rich glitter

Red, Orange, Yellow, Green, Blue, Indigo and Violet = ornate, gold-edged rainbow, genuinely lovelier…large, genuinely lovelier rainbow: denoted God…I elate digger under one lovely golden rainbow…give all, get one, genuinely ordered, old rainbow…one rainbow-end unveiler, all to gold-digger eye

Red Scare = red races

Refuse to Play Wimbledon = superbly flawed emotion

Reincarnation = an incinerator…I to an inner arc

Republican Party = capably prurient

The Republican Party = try neat, happier club…petty, banal, pure rich…aren't public therapy…entire rat club happy…I enter happy rat club…I enter rat club, happy…pure planetary bitch…buy that pearl, Prince…reputably, in the crap…authentic pearl by PR…puny, pathetic barrel…clear, unhappy, bitter…the purer PC banality…reach abruptly inept…the aberrancy pulpit…crap elephant, bury it…prat Cheney: April tub…they: a public partner…Palin: a pretty cherub?

Religion = groan, lie…no girlie…le origin…I, one girl…I, iron leg

Rent-A-Car = ran trace…race rant

Resist = sister

Restaurant = eat rats, run

Rest in Peace = sane receipt…is neat creep

Retractions = to recant, sir

Revenge of the Sith = event: heroes fight

Revolution = love to ruin

Rhinestones = note shiners

Ripley's Believe It or Not = is lovely, bitter pioneer…lively enterprise, boo it?

Roast Turkey = try our steak

Rock and Roll Hall of Fame = all of the charm and folklore

Roland Garros = ran lord or gas…Lord, ran so rag…or grand solar…oar-lords rang…or gnarl roads…or radar's long…lard or groans…lag rods or ran…god roar, snarl

Roll in the Hay = thrill a honey

Roman Catholic Priest = to preach to criminals…a complainer to Christ…hit sermonic crap a lot

Roman Empire = I'm an Emperor

The Roman Empire = hot, mean premier

Romeo and Juliet = mated junior, ole…la mort d'une joie…one jilted amour…lure me to adjoin…one jade turmoil…true lie and mojo

Romeo and Juliet by William Shakespeare = horrible Italian jealousy deems pm wake…I'll make play jibe with amorous serenade…the jealous libido makes war in mere play…shall I kill ideal joy between paramours?

Romeo and Juliet, William Shakespeare's = Oh, Jesus! well, I'm a dreamlike separation

Rome Was Not Built in a Day = any labour I do wants time

Rome Wasn't Built in a Day = but laid in two years, man…but nor was Medina, Italy…A.D. Italian town by Remus…but, Italians may wonder

Rosetta Stone = reason to test

Roswell and the Aliens = swellhead on latrines

Roswell Incident = nerds will notice

The Roswell UFO Incident = would hint on secret file…would hint: No Secret File!

Royal Mail Postal Service = I may lose parcels to rival

Royal Military Academy, Sandhurst = Army trained duty as scholarly aim

Rumble in the Jungle = injure hell-bent mug

Russian = in a USSR

Russian Revolution = Oui, our Lenin vs. Tsar…no evil, ruinous Tsar…O, revulsion at ruins

The Russian Revolution = no virtuous Stalin here…later rush Soviet Union…result: Soviet Union, rah…Lenin routs the savior…the USSR, our evil nation…Oh, rates virtuous Lenin…the over-ruinous Stalin…Oh, our venture is Stalin…State in revulsion hour…Lenin: he's tutor, savior…O, hovels unite, ruin Tsar…Oh unite, so evil Tsar run

Revolution in Russia = a sour, evil intrusion…it's Lenin, our Saviour!

The Russian Federation = free unit: no tsar us head…dis unions that are free?

Rudolph, The Red-Nosed Reindeer = deplored, he is the odder runner

Russian Roulette = to insure a result…unusual or interest…unserious rattle…O, result ain't sure

Saint Elmo's Fire = rise into flames…is lit for seamen

Saint Louis = I is no Tulsa

Saint Paul's Cathedral = arched, palatial stuns

St. Paul's Cathedral = castrated phallus…dust, altar, chapels…adult star's chapel…has a sculpted altar

Sanitarium = I am a nut, sir

Satan = Santa

Satanic = a sin act

Satanism = ain't mass

Satan Lucifer = careful saint?

Satisfaction Guaranteed = I rate café as outstanding…I'd rent fat sausage action…fat organ in sauciest date…tart fed in sausage action…I in, a fat nude escort, a stag

Saturday Night Live = it's a naughty drivel...raised TV, naughtily...I advert tiny laughs...has vulgar identity...laughter in TV, I'd say...handiest vulgarity

Saturn = sun rat...nu star...sun art...stun Ra...turn as... a turns...runs at

Saturn's Moon Titan = not star mountains...transmutation son...no transmutations...O no mutant strains

Say It With Flowers = so we flirt this way...it's worth wife's lay...swiftly with a rose...hostility, few wars...list wife as worthy...why wait for it less?

School Cafeteria = hot, cereal fiasco

Science-Fiction = once scientific

Scientology = isn't ecology...yes, not logic...Incestology...in costly ego

Church of Scientology = goofy, rich-chosen cult...rich con's goofy cult, eh?

Search-Engines = reaching sense?

Sears Tower = worst rates

Seattle Seahawks = weak-ass athletes

Seattle, Washington = he's gettin' a slow tan...hating wetness a lot

Seclusion = close us in

Second City = do cynic set

Secret Agent = center stage

Secret Police = erectile cops

Secret Service = receives crest

Secret World of Anagrams = *arrogant defamers scowl*

Seeing a Shrink = shrieking sane

Seinfeld = ends life…snide elf…I end self

Self-Satisfaction = O, I finest lass. fact!

Serial Killer = earlier kills…Israel killer…is real killer…kill realizer…I, laser killer

Serial Mom = semi-moral

Seven Year Itch = nasty vice here…I envy cheaters

Sex and the City = next day ethics

Siemens = nemesis

Sixth Sense = next hisses

Sears Roebuck and Co. = scores coke, a U.S. brand

Semolina = is no meal

Separation = one is apart

Seven Eleven Incorporated = open it and never ever close

Sexual Harassment = shame transsexual…shames natural sex

Sexual Intercourse = our lust, an exercise…is extraneous cruel…routine, secular sex…exults in a resource…unserious excretal…stereo luxuriances…neat luxuries score…curious, tense, relax…erect luxuries: a son

Sgt. Peppers Lonely Hearts Club Band = crap LP sung by the LSD-prone Beatles

Sliced Bread = edible cards

Smith and Wesson = own this? madness!

Shakespeare in Love = heaven-like as prose…heaven likes a poser

Shamanism = I smash man

Shamrock = charms OK

Shooting Heroin = on snootier high

Silent = listen

Silicon Graphics = a long chip crisis…can logic slip, sir?

Singer = reigns

Singin' in the Rain = hit in, in earnings

Sith Toys = so shitty

Sixth Floor of the Texas School Book Depository = foxes look for hot blood. hope this story is exact

Skin Cancer = scar in neck

Skin Care = irks acne…risk acne

Sleeping Together = get their legs open

Slot Machines = cash lost in me…ha, smelt coins…cash lost in 'em…the manic loss…slim, no cheats…scam in hotels

Smile, You're on Candid Camera = my American audience drools

Snakes on the Plane = sneak on elephants

Snort Cocaine = consecration…narcotic ones…narcotic nose…nice cartoons

Snooze Alarms = alas, no more Zs

Soap Opera = oops, a rape

Solitary Confinement = I fear I'm only contents...lone time in frosty can...often stoney criminal...controls meanie, nifty...it's my felon container...confirm entity's alone...finest, tiny, clean room...Mr. Finite, solo tenancy...for men in a tiny closet...infernal comes to tiny...notice male in Y-fronts

Somewhere in Time = I, the new memories

Somewhere Over the Rainbow = worrisome however beneath

Sordid Details = dildo disaster

Soul Mate = same lout

South Africa = ah, fractious

South America = I am true chaos

Southern California = life in a car or hot sun

Space Shuttle Atlanta = latest launch, past tea?

Space Shuttle Atlantis = the stainless catapult...that pile: the last US ascent...last in these catapults...spelt a last act in the US...pass the tile test at launch...that suits planet scale...spelt, sat at launch site?

Space Shuttle Challenger = *the ascent, gasp. cruel hell!*

Space Shuttle Challenger Launch = cheapest hull, ungallant screech

The Space Shuttle Challenger = the huge spectacle enthralls...the large stealth clenches up

The Challenger Disaster = the careless darling

Space Shuttle Columbia = *mishap but locate clues...chaotic tumble US pales...is a comet thus culpable?*

The Space Shuttle Columbia = humble, pathetic lost cause...the meticulous, cheap blast!

The Space Shuttle Columbia Re-Entry = true catastrophe, belches untimely...the cruelest botchery manipulates...true, hesitant computer bellyaches

Space Shuttle Discovery = epic thrust solves decay...USS Scotch Tape delivery...shitty clouds serve Cape

The Launch of Discovery = heavy conflicted hours...huh, scary device loft, no?

Space Shuttle Discovery's Last Launch = NASA cuts the loud travel-ships cycle

Space Shuttle Endeavour = couldn't have repeat uses...leave up at decent hour...unseated US travel epoch...a US venture lasted, epoch...ascent let US up overhead...USA apt never to schedule...the US cut NASA developer...a vested Earth uncouples...Oh, seven sure catapulted...so cluttered-up a heavens...*seven-death capsule tour*...so, the capsule adventure...leaves Cape, thunders out

Endeavour Ends Final Mission with the Smooth Landing = so main Shuttle now home and finished in doing travels

Shuttle Ready to Dock with Space Station = Atlantis decreed to touch with a sky-post

Space, the Final Frontier = in search of life-pattern...Life, respect, faith ran on...this off-center airplane...ran on Life, respect, faith...in craft, no past life here...E.T. in real inept crash off...I can halt off Enterprise...Lor trip has inane effect...I perfect one flash train...O, feel a frantic sprint, eh?

The Final Frontier = or ninth afterlife

Space Tourism = I come up stars

Space Travel = re: vast place

Spaghetti Sauce = his 'get pasta' cue

Spaghetti Western = West theatre's ping...theatre signs wept...ten greatest whips

Spain = pains...a spin

Spandex = expands

Spanish Armada = mad as piranhas

Special Delivery Stamps = price vastly speeds mail

Spectra = ET's crap

Spirits of the Dead = this is of departed

Sports Bra = traps orbs

Springer Show = press whoring

Spring, Summer, Autumn, Winter = "times running past," we murmur

Stage Act = get a cast

Stage Fright = fret, gag, shit

Starbuck's Coffee = bet for café, sucks

Star Wars = raw stars...rats wars

Star Wars Episode One: The Phantom Menace = space as entertainment? whoops, dear me...remade phenomenon is catastrophe, waste...set prior to 'A New Hope,' same man ascendeth...handsome Emperor's won apathetic Senate...ashamed Portman, Neeson were so pathetic...Neeson, a master showpiece, hated Portman

Star Wars Episode Three = whore repeats disaster

Star Wars Trilogy = LA artistry grows...warty rigors last

State of the Union Address = dishonest data? sure, often...United

States herd on sofa...head for United States, son...use father's dated notions...tuned softheads set on-air...so, father tuned-in set, soda...FAO interested thousands...strident tones of USA head...US nation: 'e heed draft toss...fathead onto US residents

The State of the Union Address = threats do not defeat Hussein...see, he's no fathead, I don't trust...eh, USA intends to test for hard...and so I see the stunt of hatred...or shit-headed stunt of Senate...set fire, no to U.N. deaths, deaths...OTT stunt of airhead, he's dense...he fans the United States odor...feeds on deaths: that's routine...O, he's enthused if data's rotten...the United States honors fade...he's set to defraud the nations...USA, its dense Head to the front...detest then, for its USA head, no?

Statue of Liberty = by a tourist fleet...a style of tribute...Abe felt your tits...I flatter you best...luster to beautify...beauty itself? rot...it free U.S. by total...Ol' feet a bit rusty...built to stay free?

The Statue of Liberty = your tablet fits thee...to thy better U.S. life...thirty feet: absolute...soft-lit beauty there...i.e. Sole, but hefty tart...a better life to thy US...yet oft belies a truth

Steadily Rising Oil Price = spirit rose daily, ceiling?

Stella Artois = stale rat's oil...stale rat soil...rat's stale oil...rat's toil ales

Stella Artois Appreciation Society = pet spit! it's an atrocity! I choose real ale

Stenographer's Handiwork = a peg workers in shorthand

Stephen King Novel = pen invokes length

Stilettos = toe stilts

Stipend = spent it

Stormy Weather = may throw trees...warm? yes, hotter

Story of Christ = thirty of cross...this cry, sort-of

Strike Three = hitters reek

String Theory = trying others

Striptease = see tit, rasp…a tits spree…tapestries…peer tit, ass…I stare, pets…tape sister

Striptease Clubs = braless tits, puce…it beats Scruples…as testicles burp

Stuart Little = title: rat lust

Sub-Atomic Particle = impact? orbit's a clue

Submarine = buries man

Sumo Wrestling, Japanese Sport of = lot of gross men, just wear nappies…wrap us men for pose, giants jostle

Sunset Boulevard = burned out slaves

Super Bowl Sunday = brawl? yes, pound us

Super Massive Black Hole = misshape lovable sucker

Supreme Court = computer user…corrupt? sue me!

Surfing the Internet = fringe interest hunt

Surgical Instruments = smart, curing utensils

Sweet Smile = we timeless

Switzerland = waltz is nerd…Lizards went…waltzer's din…wizard's Lent…waltz Red sin…lizard newts…wander Liszt…lizard 'n stew

Symbionese = boy nemesis

Sympathy for the Devil = play this over-fed myth

Take Me Out to the Ballgame = make athlete out to gamble

Talk is Cheap = ha, skeptical

Tantrums = must rant

Teletubbies = best tube lie

Television = TV is one lie…it's evil one…it's one evil…it vile ones…evilest ions…note: is evil…note: is vile…note: is live…I note evils…sit, evil one…one evil, sit…is evil tone…tone is evil…on site, live…it evil ones…it nose evil…no levities…in evil toes

Television, Cable = bestial violence…noticeable evils…live, obscene tail

Cablevision = is viable con

Television, Daytime = O, I deem it vile, nasty…I live on steamy diet…O man, I eyed live tits…veto media senility…timely video nastie…O, it is my ideal event…violent? seedy? I am it…tiny, emotive ladies…steamy, evil edition…O man, it vile, seedy…media is not yet vile?

Television, Freeview = interviewees of evil…even wee frivolities…in live: we foresee ITV

Television Networks = knew violent stories…OK, Western is violent…Western is not live, OK?

Television Set = see, it's not live…it sees violent…tie to vileness…it is steel oven…it is tense love

Television Sitcoms and Soap Operas = advertise non-stop. Omo is a special

Ten Commandments = most men can't mend

The Ten Commandments = comments that end men…them contents damn me

Tennis = net's in…intens…in nets…is 'n net…ten sin…set inn

Tennis Ball = blast 'n line…balls in net

Tennis Court = instruct one…curt tension

Tennis Game = net enigmas…Enigma nets

The Game of Tennis = the enigma of the nets

Tesla Coil = oscillate

Texas Holdem = sex-mad hotel

That's One Small Step For a Man, One Giant Leap For Mankind, Neil Armstrong = an Eagle lands on Earth's Moon, making a first small permanent footprint…an Earthman landing on Moon speaks, meaning all profit later from tests…NASA sent man along to the Moon, making PR lift for lame President R.N., alas…message from a flight to Moon, a pennant still marks an open land terrain…one man marks range, one man pats flag, third one (left in Apollo) transmits…fatal start: stepping on far Moon harms (killed) a gnome alien, no remnants…gentleman sprang off a starship and sent an emotional moral to Kremlin…Apollo mission marks a milestone fanfare that grand long-term pennant…mission report: a tall, metal pennant marks a damn fine golf shot on range…poor folk ate dirt as NASA management men spent ransom on ill-ran flight…thin man ran, left planet, makes a large stride, pins flag on Moon…on to Mars…the Moon is made of green Parmesan, Martian folk start planning stall, no?

That's One Small Step for Man, One Giant Leap for Mankind = famed Neil Armstrong on pleasant Moon path talks fine

The Acquired Immune Deficiency Syndrome = conquered misery if much-needed intimacy…I'm chief mystique or undermine decadency…yummier homicides in frequent decadency…I'm queer incendiary of much-needed mystic…I'm a chief murdered mystique on indecency

The American Free Press = I'm a sharpest reference

The American Nazi Party = terminate in a hazy crap

The American Revolution = our achievement on trial…much tea in one river, a lot…elation: much tea on river…to hire maniac volunteer…O, arm each volunteer in it

The Anagram Code = not game charade…gotcha name, dear…to dream a change

The Anglican Church = arch nag cliché hunt

The Answer to Life, the Universe and Everything = the adventure-writing, finest heavenly heroes…anywhere of true, light-hearted inventiveness…fine sweethearts or unevenly thieving hatred…Earthly unwashed frightens retentive Evil One

The Apollo Moon Landing = Neil along to hold map, no?

The First Moon Landing = Earthling's foot 'n mind…of Aldrin's men tonight…*grand hit on film-set, no?*

America's First Moon Landing = grand-scale misinformation…California sand, strong mime…damn farce mission, grin a lot…a mad Sci-Fi, no Neil Armstrong?

NASA Faked the Moon Landings = fans asked to hang on damn lie…hang onto damn lies and fakes

The Arabian Desert = it's a heated barren

The Archeologist = he's got a hot relic

The Arctic Circle = chart ice circlet

The Artesian Wells = water's in all these…earnest hill sweat

The Associated Press = has editors set space

The Astral Plane = help alert Satan…a tape enthralls…all earnest path…repel Satan, halt!

Theatrical Costumes = I am art's cute clothes

The Axis Power = hoax, sweet rip…it hoax spewer…I expose wrath…hoax, wiser pest…is a show expert

The Battle at Waterloo = Oo, we'll batter that foe…O, to treat who left Elba…hot war, foe-bottle tale

Battle of Waterloo = O, belt foe, total war

Waterloo = ole to war

The Betty Ford Clinic = ditch bottle? cry: fine!

The Bible Code Revealed = the believable decoder…he led to deceive rabble

The Big Glacier = bright, large ice

The Bill of Rights = so, filth, blighter

The Billy Graham Crusade = absurd, charity Hell Game…Hell is draughty macabre

The British Crown = witch in brothers…borne with Christ?

The British Parliament = hint: the Imperial brats

The California Gold Rush = fools hunt a real rich dig

The Cannes Film Festival = flash event lifts cinema

The Carnegie Library = be literary, charge in!

The Carter Administration = that Democrat tires in Iran…that domestic Iran terrain…Iranian desert tract, I'm hot

The Carter Doctrine = or act, then redirect…then redirect actor!

The Cathedral of Notre Dame de Paris, France = dear dead architect offers phenomenal art

Cathedral of Notre Dame = a tooled French-made art…at mood, read French tale…then record tale of a mad…

Notre Dame = dare to men…men to dare…O, dern

team…Emendator

The University of Notre Dame = even I in to study there for MA

The Centuries of Nostradamus = so scan dreams into the future

The Prophecies of Nostradamus = premonished UFO catastrophes…forecasts hide upon metaphors…defuse anthropomorphic asset

The Check is in the Mail = claim, heck I sent it, heh

The Civil War = arch evil wit

The Clinton Administration = taint this old intern, Monica…slid into that intern, Monica

The Cold War = cheat world

The Countryside = no city dust here…cheers to nudity…it crude honesty…touchy resident…hey, destruction

The Crocodile Hunter = cute hero to children

The Crusades = curses! hated…curses! death…re: cuts heads…reduces hats…death curses…truces, a shed…crushed East…seduce trash…the' scared us…rudest aches…ceased hurts…the sad curse…death's sucre…cussed Earth…dutchess era…the used cars…such dearest…heads! truces!

The Customer is Always Right = cite Wal-Mart guy's horseshit…get star smile with your cash…'how much?' is retail strategy…other guy's ethic is Wal-Mart's…what's the image? courtly sirs…I suit my charge to less wrath…cash got with treasury smile…I'm way tight, cash rules store…that's: I might screw your sale…how I test retail guy's charms…such might to sway retailers…laughter? how Macy's resist it…come try this waitress, laugh…myth, laughter, 'cos I waitress…weigh truth: I'm a classy store…trust my wise Tesco girl, ah ha…High Street says: court Wilma…why I must register cash a lot…her wish rules at Macys, got it…what, thy costume is large, sir…is this how Macy's rule Target?

The Daily News = deathly swine…wealthy snide

The Daily Show = why, ideal host…yeah, wild host…why oil deaths?

The Da Vinci Code = had it conceived…hidden act o' vice…voice act, hidden…voiced and ethic…the candid voice…do divine cashet…I'd have cited con…convicted, die, ha…addictive con, eh?

The Da Vinci Code by Dan Brown = odd cheat, now binned by vicar

Da Vinci Code = candid voice…add vice icon

The Dawning = night waned

The Devil = the lived…idle TV, eh?

The Discovery of America = i.e. chase victory of dream

The Donner Party = hyper and rotten

The DuPont Corporation = not pothead, corruption

The Early Bird Catches the Worm = able theory charmed twitchers…why, the critter adores AM belch

The Earthquakes = that queer shake

The Economy = oh, money, etc…

The Eiffel Tower = O feet! where lift?

The Electric Car = rather eclectic

The End of the Line = hint of the needle…if hot needle, then…the hot fin' needle…of the thin needle…the fine hotel end

The End of the World is Nigh = down this hole, frightened

End of the World = flow hot redden...red-hot 'n flowed...end red-hot wolf...deft horned owl...the wolf droned...redden, hot wolf...down threefold...fold the wonder...flow red-hot end

When Will the World End = now well withheld, nerd

The English Patient = the git's in the plane...I enlighten the past

The Exorcist = heroic texts

The Eyes = they see

The Family Circus = Life: it much scary

The Fast Food Restaurant = fat rodent treat Oh a fuss...do feature hot transfats...rats often eat out, rest as so fat, don't eat further...short feast and after: out...tour: a hot transfats feast...affronts, hardest eat-out

Fast Food Restaurant = saturated fat for son...fate: transfat odours

The Fifth Element = the tenth film fee

The Film Industry = filthy rudiments

The Cinema Industry = undermine chastity...tumidity enhancers

Cinema = M. Caine

Motion Picture = omit porn cutie

The First Men on Mars = in the monster's farm

The First World War = raw, self-worth dirt

The Florida Vote Recount = done to cover their fault

The French Revolution = over the Chunnel for it...violent hunt for cheer...court filth? no nerve, eh...love her finer hot c**t...hunt her, violent force...event left rich honour?

A French Revolution = France, violent hour…unveil Franco-throne…cheerful innovator…love for nice turn, ah…continue her flavor…turnover of each nil…loan chief turnover…incoherent flavor

French Revolution = run forth violence…Northern, voiceful

The Galileo Satellite Navigation System = it is elegantly vital as to get aliens home…one lost a Hamlet? get signal, it's vital: I, eye

The Game of Billiards = aim ball for this edge

The Game of Football = fame to the goofball

The General Electric Corporation = or ace technological interpreter

The Geneva Convention = the one 'given' covenant

The Gobi Desert = gosh, better die

The Godfather = theft, hard ego…oh, theft raged…the hated frog…the hog farted

The Godfather, Crime Drama = Mafia: get them, hard record

The God Particle Mystery = get my secret? ah, pity Lord

The Golden Globes = god, hell-bent egos…hot, belonged legs…god, the noble legs…belongs *the Lodge*

The Good News Bible = how Gentile sobbed

The Google Search-Engine = oh, cheer, net-logging ease

The Gospel According to Saint Matthew = we can depict His torments at Golgotha

The Gospel of Judas Iscariot = I trace this good pal of Jesus…I just see a good pal of Christ…his special fate just or good?…top disgrace? he is just a fool…Oh Lord, justifies scapegoat…role: he's just a good pacifist…a good pal to Jesus Christ, fie…a disciple forgot oath, Jesus!

Gospel of Judas = pal of Jesus, God…Jesus a flop God?

The Graduate = eat daughter

The Great American Novel = *entice the anagram lover*…even alarming to teacher…large achievement on art…large art achievement, no?

The Great Dictator = it graced to the Rat…it graced to threat…that redirect goat…redirect that G.O.A.T.

The Greatest = gets theatre…'e's the target

The Great Pyramid of Cheops = my god, perfect Pharaoh site

The Great War = what a regret!

The Grim Reaper = prime gatherer

The Guardian = huge, radiant…ah, rude giant…I read naught…it harangued…dart in Hague…darn it, Hague…a hit, nude rag…in a daughter…a great Hindu…a rude hating…IRA gun death

The Hand of God = Oh, doth defang

The Heimlich Maneuver = even I'm much healthier

The Holocaust = echo that soul…O, such lot hate…such loot, hate…ash clue: tooth…hath cut loose

The Holocaust History = shoot! cruelty, it Shoah…Hitler sot youth, chaos!

The Holy Grail = hail the glory…the girly halo

The Hospital Ambulance = a cab, I hustle to help man

The Hound of the Baskervilles, Sir Arthur Conan Doyle's = ah, rather nosy Sherlock hunts bad evil fiend, routs, ole…hurrah, I said, and truly one of the best Sherlock novels

The House of Representatives = thou see there a nest of vipers

The House of Windsor = wife: horse to hounds...O, we found this horse...O, shed of unworthies...we shoot doe, fish run...O, the so unwished-for

The Houses of Parliament = top man here's a foul shite...loonies far up the Thames...the shameful operations...often pushes lame hot-air...the, uh, professional team...the tearful homo sapiens...the fat homo sapiens rule...forum: 'Is not Heath asleep?'...a fearless Pitt, Hume, Hoon...aha! stop the senile forum...has lust on Empire of Hate...PM's of a hostile nature, eh?

The Hubbard Glacier = hard ice, bath bulger

The Hunchback of Notre Dame = the arch-foe, unmatched nob...a buck-toothed Frenchman

The Hunchback of Notre Dame, Written by Victor Hugo = French book about totty-mad revenge within church

The Ides of March = smirched of hate

The Immaculate Conception = no help intact cutie, come, ma...clean-cut, empathic emotion...I am the incomplete account...a cute, chemical omnipotent...pathetic cult, I mean come ON!

The Incredible Hulk = he childlike 'n brute

The Indian Ocean = had no innate ice

The Influence of Alcohol = oh hell, continual coffee

The Intel Corporation = tailor one rotten chip...a ship or Internet tool?

The Internet = enter the tin...ether in tent

The Internet Industry = intent: sturdy? neither...intent intruders, they...tiny inherent, trusted?

The Computer Industry = pure myth destruction…up then dirty customer…see much dirty porn? tut

The Irish Republican Army = relay much pain, re: British…IRA? a prime, slithery bunch…yep, I can harm British rule

The Island of Dr. Moreau = dear, lush deformation

The Jefferson Administration = framed this joint's Free Nation

The Koran = harken to

The Last of the Mohicans = oh, the stoic man has left…half heathen, most stoic

The League of Nations = a tough, neat felonies

The Leaning Tower of Pisa = when Italian, get for pose…I warn thee of giant slope…Italian hopes often grew…what a foreign stone pile…a foreign head 'e tilts now…a steep roof, angle within?

The Legislature = elite slaughter

The Life and Adventures of Nicholas Nickleby = Dickens: naïve enter fanciful Dotheboys Hall…fine tale, find thou a novel by Charles Dickens…novel by Dickens: oh, ah, real fateful incidents

The Life of Brian = fire noble faith…brief, hot finale…noble faith fire

The Liquor Habit = quit! I rob health

The Living Daylights = dashingly tight evil

The Loch Ness Monster = shh, somnolent secret…con-men hosts shelter…och, she torments lens…her, on them Scots' lens

A Monster of Loch Ness = most of clans see horn

The Lost Paradise = Earth's ideal spot…to sharp-set ideal…dearest hospital

The Lusitania = it is neat haul

The Magical Mystery Tour = ratty, mythical, gruesome...mythical, grotty measure...I am the ugly mercy to star...mutate Almighty sorcery...I am true mercy to ghastly...regrets mouthy calamity

The Matrix Reloaded = a red-hot, altered mix...loth, made extra dire...lord, the extra media...the Marx idea retold...admire red, hot Latex

The Mayan Volcano = yon lava cometh, na

The Meaning of Life = the fine game of nil...one fine, lame fight...fame? I feel nothing...feel fate homing in...Oh, game, fifteen-nil...golf, feminine heat...feeling fit? ahem, no...fine time, half gone...I, the feeling of man...effeminate holing...the offline enigma

The Menage a Trois = a giant threesome

The Middle East = smelt death, die!

The Middle East Peace Talks = ditch deals, keep stalemate...a deal template is sketched...let's sit, chat deep, make deal...Semites talked, eh? deal, pact...tied pact seemed 'all task, eh?

The Miracle on the Hudson = Shuttle-honored machine...here, humid 'can.' not lost, eh?

The Miracle Worker by William Gibson = girl whom I tame by own crib is a Keller

The Mississippi River = this is impressive rip...his impressive spirit

The Mississippi River Delta = shrimp pile as tide revisits...it is shrimp pastes I deliver...I am silt shippers revisited...shippers revisit silt I made

The Miss World Beauty Contest = brunettes mostly, so I

watched...tasty chest, rude to Women's Lib...let tits, c**t, arse embody show...modestly hot, cute breasts win...c**ts with altered bosoms, yet...not a 'select who is best' duty, Mr....old women's chesty attributes...monster double-tit chest sway...study Charline's sweet bottom...both out? my dress-elastic went...hint: we assorted comely butts...worthless, mutated obscenity...badly written, those costumes...warm hedonists, busty Colette...to teach studs women's liberty...old women's chesty attributes...custom: we brainless totty, eh?

The Mister Universe Contest = monster chest, I venture

The Monuments of Mars = softer, human moments...sneer of mammoth stun...sneer of t' mammoth Sun...torment of human mess...met monsters of human

The Moon = not home...O, then om...moo, then...he not mo...ho to men...Toho men...O, met hon

Moon = no mo

The Moon is Made from Green Cheese = son hee-heed fromage-mice monster...ah, Tesco men mine her: food emerges

The Morse Code = here come dots

The Murders in the Rue Morgue, by Edgar Allan Poe = you remember, one ape hurt and slaughtered girl

The Mystery of Amelia Earhart = the fatal air...the Memory Years...aerial safety, that her memory?

The Mystery Writers of America's Edgar = yes, their reward system for great crime

The NASA Mars Exploration Rover Mission = O Roman planet has visitors or examiners...O roams: horn proves alien Martians exist!

The NASA Space Shuttle Discovery = evades catastrophe in such style...ecstasy to see launch pads thrive...evade loss in trusty escape hatch…spy cased the astronaut's vehicle

The National Weather Service Forecast = chief event alert, wear those raincoats

The Nazi Regime = I'm eager zenith

The Nobel Prize for Literature = a terrible one for the Pulitzer?

The Nuclear Regulatory Commission = your rules clone atomic nightmares!

The Nude in Art = nature hinted…it underneath

The Office = hit coffee

The Oldest Profession = denotes hole's profits…first step: do one's holes…so pose, fondle her tits…fetidness, poor hotels

The Old Man and the Sea = hat lamented, no shade…hothead man ends tale

The Old West = who settled

Theoretical Physics = critical hypothesis…hypothetical crisis…Oh, I scythe particles…hey, Catholic priests…this teacher's policy

The Oscars = chose star…has escort…so: cast her…ah, escorts…oh, actress…she, actors…cast heros…casts hero…she co-star…horses act…horse acts…SOS her act…ohs, reacts…reacts, soh…hot caress…scare host…chest oars…host races…has corset…chose arts…echo stars…och, stares…shear cost…he's actors…those cars…hers, coats…so cheat'rs…to Cher ass…hate cross…she or arts ecast hos…corse hats…her acts so…act hero SS

The Academy Awards = what ace daydreams…watch a seedy drama…a dame-watchers day…what? a dream decays…watches a daydream…award a chesty dame…easy-watched drama…cameras had wet day…dear acted, way hams…day we dear hams act...Mayer was hated cad...Hamadryads' wee act...way dear hams acted...whaddya set? camera!

Academy Awards = drama saw decay...a sacred, mad way

Academy Awards Nominations = aim named: win an Oscar today...or as day in a cinema-mad town

The Oscar Nomination = it's not a cinema honor

Academy of Motion Picture Arts and Sciences = studs of cinema anticipated Oscar ceremony...my nice Media coup: attend fine actors' Oscars

The Outer Oort Belt = robot outlet there...robot ether outlet...let turbo ether too

The Passion = saint hopes...as phoniest?

The Passion of Jesus Christ = just the pain of his crosses

The Passion of the Christ = Oh, spot theist franchise

The Pastries = pies, tarts, eh

The Paths of Glory Lead But to the Grave = the poet Gray doubts that Hell forgave

The Pen is Mightier than the Sword = the emphasis, then, red-hot writing...here's hating the inept wordsmith...tight phrase method wins therein...I win, tight phrases dethrone them...the right words shape eminent hit...how arm strength hides in epithet

The People's Republic of China = open chip shop, eat rice, be full

The Republic of China = the pail of rice bunch...input of rice, ah, belch

The Pillsbury Dough Boy = hi, behold burly guy's pot

The Planet Earth = elephant threat...the eternal path

The Planets = the ten pals

The Playboy Centerfold = behold only pretty face...beyond perfect, tally-ho!

The Postmaster General = he's letter-post manager

The Premature Burial, by Edar Allan Poe = ah, tell Grim Reaper: be up and about early!

The Price is Right = tight, Irish creep

The Price of Fame = empathic fee for...emphatic fee for?

The Priory of Sion = poor history? fine...fine, poor history...their spoof: irony

The Promised Land = spin the old dream...the damn lie drops...a splendid mother...amid the splendor...the miser pod land...to splendid harem...so, the dream held pint?

The Public Art Galleries = large picture halls, I bet

The Railroad Train = hi, I rattle and roar

The Rat Race = that career

The Raven, by Edgar Allan Poe = aha! a bender! rap gently, love...heavenly Bard, page to turn

The Red Sea = the erased

There Is a God in Heaven = overhead shine in gate

There Is Plenty of Water on the Moon, NASA Confirms = Oh man, in front of planet Earth, *we see moist son cry*

The Republic of Ireland = Bertie Ahern lucid? flop...chief ale: Dublin Porter...fear Dublin hotel price...I belch fine auld porter...free? Britain could help...I retold Leprechaun fib...Bertie Ahern could flip...Freda: 'Cheerio Punt Bill'...O, bullet Erin chap fired...Erin rifle chap bled out...Dublin PO: rifle act here...pub for the idle in Clare…Dublin PO rifle teacher…place in direful bother…hire Dublin Forte place…land of epic Britain rule, eh?

The Resurrection = O Christ, U reenter…torture enriches?

The Rings of Saturn = unearths frosting…turn forth in gases

The Rocky Mountains = I'm the contours, Yank

The Roland Garros Tournament in Paris, France = R. Nadal, rather again, performs on tennis court

The Royal Opera House = lousy repartee, hoo-ha…yo-ho-ho, a true pleaser

The Sahara Desert = dearest heat rash…heat rash, dearest

The Saint Louis Arch = nautical horseshit

The Salem Witch Trials = this celestial warmth…celestial warmth hits

Salem Witch Trials = is ace, still warmth…is warm still cheat…it claims wrathless…wills castrate him…well, is that racism?

The Salvation Army = note vast Hail Mary…O, hymn art's alive, ta…I am they lover, Satan…or salivate at hymn…e, I am thy Satan lover

The Satanic Bible = isn't ethical, babe

The Satanic Verses = scares the natives…Christ! nice ass, Eve!

The Sears Tower = we are the shortest…a whore's street

The Second World War = not chewed warlords

The Shadow Cabinet = oh, bewitched Satan…new death cohabits

The Shawshank Redemption = he saw them, thanked prison…time the posh wanker's hand

The Shoe Manufacturer = ouch, a man's feet-hurter

The Shroud of Turin = truths, if honoured...if truths undo hero...if the hot, surround...hero is found truth...truth if honored us...nourished of truth...if rude truths, oh no

The Sign of the Cross = he's right to confess

The Simpsons = men's hot piss...most hipness...the simps' son...Ms. Shit opens...honest simps

The Simpsons, a Cartoon = a spot shot on Americans

The Simpsons Cartoons = spastic Homer, snot son

The Itchy and Scratchy Show = on which Rat scythed shy Cat

The Silence of the Lambs = the con bites male flesh...FBI: he's mean to the cells...to belch, I eat men's flesh...best meal? nice, hot flesh...FBI meets con, he's lethal...meal fetish, belch on set...belch on meatiest flesh...a flesh comestible then?

The Sistine Chapel = the speech is Latin...it helps 'ace' the sin...silence is the path...hint: ethics please

The Sopranos = a person shot...shooters' nap...hot personas

The Sound of Music = seduction of hums...hum of disco tunes...fun duets, I smooch...funds come, I shout

The Spanish Armada = tar: "ships ahead, men"...meant as a hardship...smash a pirate hand...smashed in a trap, ah...hard at ship, seaman...hardship at sea, man...am Death's piranhas

The Spirit of Saint Louis = his feat is solo-unit trip...his unit feat is solo trip...hot plane is ours, is it fit?

The Spy Who Loved Me = show lymph devotee...wholesome, hyped TV

The Stanley Cup Final = let fans hunt ice play...that playful niceness

The Star Spangled Banner = grant a resplendent bash…bars lend a pen strength…planted as brethren sang…breathless and pregnant…bands help arrange tents…grabs pennant, hard steel…handle pregnant breasts…greatest land, brash Penn…led, pennant grabs hearts…handle pregnant breasts…blest pennant has regard…bash transparent legend…bars lend a pen a strength

The State of Israel = foes are latest hit…retaliates soft, eh?

State of Israel = settler of Asia…a flat, sore site

The Story of Christ = thrifty hero costs…hero's thrifty cost

The Submarine Warfare = fine, rare, water ambush

The Swinging Sixties = sin, getting sex? I wish

The Sydney Opera House = yo, espouse Haydn there

The Tabloids = oh, bad titles

The Talmund = ahem, nut ltd.

The Texas Chainsaw Massacre = a man with axe chases actress

The Third Reich = the direr hitch

The Dire Hitch = hid rich teeth

The Third World War = the raw Third World

The Thirteen Original Colonies = one coalition retireth English

The Time Machine = I meet hi-tech man

The Titanic, Sinking of the = hitting of ice sank it then?

Titanic, the Unsinkable Ship = in that pitiable clankiness…it isn't saintlike, punchable

The Tobacco Industry = cancer to shut-in body…tout: cancer hits body…botchy tar seduction…a botchy destruction…counteract this body…bad scent to your itch

The Cigarette and Tobacco Industry = death by cancer, to distinct outrage…they get doubt at cancer indicators

The U.S. Tobacco Industry = authentic, busy doctors?

The British Tobacco Industry = cancer! it hit robust body. shit!

The Towering Inferno = enter hot wing on fire…not worth fire engine

The Treason of Benedict Arnold = lo none defend the traitor scab

The Typewriter = write pretty, eh?

The U.S. Car Industry = shady in structure…hurts user and city

The American Automotive Industry = my variation: Detroit eunuchs, mate

The U.S. Motor Industry = Oh my, run, Detroit's shut!

The U.S. Open = oh, up teens

The U.S. War on Terror = torture shown? rare

The Video Game Industry = media diverts the young

Video Game Industry = over-imagined study…toy as drug: dive in me!

The Vietnam War = I'm a wrath event

The Village People = allege: vile pop

The Walking Dead Episodes = pang: we dislike those dead

The War Against Terrorism = I am the strangest warrior

The War in Iraq = win, hire Qatar…threw an Iraqi…win Qatar heir…earn with Iraq…Qatar, I win her

The War on Terrorism = mirror a hot Western…terrain's worth more…the warrior monster…er, wither moron rats

The Washington Monument = oh, what stunning memento

The Washington Post = ah, spotting hot news…ah, tonight's top news

The Winter Olympic Games = what is merely competing?

The World Is Not Enough = oh, one stud won the girl…gun-totin' hero led show…new delights to honour…uh, old, not worth seeing…this good whore tunnel

The World of Tomorrow = flow red-hot tomorrow…two-fold or worth more…tomorrow, red-hot wolf?

The World Series = the weird losers

The X Factor = Fox chatter

Three's Company = hepaysrent.com

Three Sheets to the Wind = the twit here, he's stoned

'Til Death Do Us Part = that stupid ordeal…total despair, thud!

Time Capsule = I'm a tin cup

Times Square, New York City = it quite rocks my New Years

Time and Tide Wait for no Man = notified madman into water

To Be Your Valentine = I, yet none but a lover

To Boldly Go Where No Man Has Gone Before = we ogle the gals onboard, be on form, honey…ha, hero begs fellow to range beyond Moon

To Cast Pearls Before Swine = one's labor is perfect waste

Today is the First Day of the Rest of Your Life = oft I'd satisfy the desire of your heart to fly

Tom and Jerry = joy, end Mr. Rat

Tom and Jerry Cartoons = or modern cat 'n rat joys…rodent story can major

Tomorrow Never Dies = reword it, Mr. O-O-Seven…wonder resort movie

Tongue in Cheek = genuine, to heck

Tony Awards = rowdy Satan…now, star day

Too Close to the Sun = not coolest, hot use

Torture Chamber = terror, beat much?

Total Eclipse = top celestial…to still peace…optical steel…satellite cop

Total Eclipse of the Moon = I'm that fool on telescope

Total Eclipse of the Sun = planets' silhouette, foc'…upshot, often celestial…hoist, flaunt telescope…O, spot the celestial fun

To Thine Own Self Be True = now utter honest belief…now feel honest tribute

Toyota Motor Corporation = O, O, too-tarty car promotion

Toys 'R' Us = so rusty

Transcendental Meditation = to LSD, an acid entertainment…detects internal damnation

Transgressions = as stronger sins

Trans World Airlines = slid narrow latrines

Trayvon Martin's Death = shot native and martyr

Treasure Island = unreal disaster…rest under a sail…tuned rear sails...natural desires

Tree of Knowledge of Good and Evil = God grew food in Eden, Eve took fall

True Christianity = a trusty INRI ethic

Trust Me = mutters

Truth Is = it hurts

Turkey Day = eat dry, yuk

Twenty Thousand Leagues Under the Sea = huge water tale stuns, end had you tense

Under George W. Bush = bugger's nude whore

Union of Soviet Socialists Republic = split is cause of countries' oblivion...basic uses of revolution in politics...policies of revolution? Cuba insists...politics of invasion, sluice out rebs...is inconceivable fortuitous spoils...if politics abusive, censor solution...so labour-intensive is politic focus...fluorescent politicians is obvious...fine politics to labour viciousness...out-of-place Leninist obvious crisis...is previous ballot if conscientious...invisible out-of-step conscious liar...boo Leninist faculties piscivorous...boo Stalinist of precious inclusive...nice isolationist of previous clubs...October politicians' useful visions...October's fine to suspicious villain...labour councils poison festivities...spurious obsolescent vilification...boo, it is up in collective of Russians...sub-process infelicitous violation...bravo, clueless fictitious opinions...oblivious, sinister self-occupation...it is unprofitable, vicious coolness...if socio-political unobtrusiveness...boss Putin: civilize Aeroflot cousin...invisible, out-of-step conscious liar...O fie, boo evil Russian c**ts' politics...Boris: sinful, vicious Police State, no?

Russia = USA air...US airs...I, a USSR...USA, sir!

Russia, America = I am scarier USA

Soviet Union = O, UN veto is in

United = untied

The United Nations = the USA, I intend not...no, it ain't enthused...the intent? do in USA...it isn't undone hate

United Nations Security Council = stoic unity, discontinue nuclear?

United States of America = dine out, taste a Mac, fries...face it, statue is no dream...aim it at us, confederates...I'm Castro-infatuated, see...I see fun, so I am attracted...made treaties count, as if...true ass, made Titanic foe...eat our Fascist dementia...attain sauciest freedom...if Democrats nauseate it...I muse, fear not, taste acid...meet our fantastic ideas...fantastic idea? sure, to me...tasted fierce Osama unit...O, neat crime data, use fist...O France made its statue...meat, fat, no rice: USA's diet...fat roasted meat cuisine...an armistice? to us, defeat...a farce, same destitution...a freedom at issue, intact...fears education at times...most cities feature an ad...dare set automatic fines...a fate came to industries...it can sue to deter Mafias...M.I.T. a neat ace for studies...atomic data use isn't free...atomic tests are fun idea...I meet Arafat's seduction...Sam: it's a cute Federation...constitutes a media fear...Canada time, tourist fees...I mandate a fist to secure...duties Monica, eat faster...Monica's diet, a true feast

The United States of America = ethnics? a fearsome attitude...the dream: fine cause, toast it...that intermediate of causes...it authenticates as freedom...a neo-fascism attitude there...a nice mass of attitude there...attitude there? O, a scam's fine...a fast coitus dementia there...defeats: no use it arithmetic...neurotic, meatiest fatheads...unerotic, meatiest fatheads...the famed, tenacious artiste...I'm state-of-the-art audiences...not safe, met a suicide threat...outcast free men aid atheist...freedom's acute anti-atheist...a hitter's automatic defense...feast, dine out, eat their Macs...cut meat, if not, heart disease...daftest authorities menace...the idea is fat c**ts eat more…traumatizes the defecation…made the treaties count? as if…that intermediate of causes…meta-truths in a sea of deceit…a frenetic madhouse, I attest…estate of Adams, in it: the cure…the tree faced out, as man I sit…the deceit is a man of stature…I teach Freemasons' attitude…the idea: Mona's face utters it…I feast, I eat the cream donuts…duties: teach man to eat fries…I made a unit of the of the tesseract…I feast the education master…if a true mate, I'd chosen a test…I teacher, state duties of man…a site enacted, shut for a time…I am a secret seed of that unit…their fates is to the educated man…a time, a fate, US to need Christ…I sent a comet Feratu: is death…so much in a tea fee started it…Osama faced institute there…deceit, threat, animus of East…ethnic Osama? defeats it: true…at true Defense, Osama hits it?

The USA = hate us

The US of A = a hot fuse…fat house…hates UFO!

The United States = the tastiest nude…the tide at sunset…untied the tastes

The Great United States of America = fattiest, true-hearted egomaniacs

The United States Government = ton invested, huge treatments…get those deviant nutters, men

Made in United States of America = created as men of U. Sam created

Made in the USA = the dim nausea…ashamed? unite!

The U.S. Library of Congress = it's only for research bugs

Union = I, no U.N.

United States Air Force = its defter aeronautics

United States Air Force Academy = academics; a fine, steady torture…education? read: 'Systematic Fear'…U.S. cadet tries aerodynamic feat…true aim? easy, cadets fornicated…I say, mate, rude cadets fornicate…defend America, Russia yet to act

Universal Studios = industrious slave…sound, visual rites…is run as video lust

Unsightly = ugly hints

Upholsterers = restore plush

Used Car = raced us

US Forces in Iraq = conquers, is fair

Using Steroids = gross nudities…so grind tissue…it is gross nude…noisiest drugs…senior disgust…disguise snort…in sore disgust

Valentine Poems = pen mates in love

Valentine's Day = a venal destiny…any valid teens…a lady-sin event…nets naïve lady

Valley Forge = yell of grave…very ole flag

Vanilla Ice Cream = all-American vice

Vatican = vain act…I vacant

Venus DeMilo = I, me unsolved

Via Satellite = at least, I live…I LIVE, at least

Victoria Secret = coercive artist…erotic star vice…carve eroticist…erotic vice arts

Victoria's Secret Catalogue = cutest, categorical ovaries…average cost: a cute clitoris…our erotic cast? it's cleavage

Volkswagon = van glow, OK

Volunteer Fire Departments = run to divert flame ere spent

Waco Stand-Off = now of sad fact…scoff own data…now scoff data…was of daft con

Walls of Jericho = for local Jewish

War and Peace = crap and a wee

War Games = wage arms

War of the Worlds = few hot warlords

War Zone = now raze

Washing Machine = shh, new magician

Washington = hating snow…hogs want in

Washington DC = don't shag in WC

Water Companies = moan, waste price…spewn to America…nice as tapeworm…impotence as war…now pirates came

Waterworld = lord, wet war…wet warlord

Weapons of Mass Destruction = U.S. team swoops, finds no trace…U.N. inspectors saw a doom-fest…U.N. inspectors: doom? 'twas safe…USA damns too few inspectors…atomic snoopers waste funds…despots set in famous war con…U.S. tosspot's war, made fine con…oft postwar mendaciousness…in fact, U.S. dope-arses own most

We are the Champions = cheers, when I am a' top

Weather Vanes = ah, veer at N.E.S.W.

Website = wise bet

Webster's Dictionary = certainties by words…ascribe word's entity…words, by certain ties…it cites nearby words

Weight Watchers = chew, waste girth

Weird Nightmares = thing we dream, sir

Western Union = no wire unsent

What Happened at Pearl Harbor = paper-partner death-blow, ha, ha

What Happened at Roswell = that hallowed newspaper

White Christmas = mister with cash…miss with her act…term is with cash…wish-time charts…that's wish-crime…the rich mass wit…i.e. thwart schism…warmth? shit, ices!

White House, Katrina = ha, authorities knew!

White House, Washington DC = down with once highest USA…inside thug, how he acts now…inside thug, he who acts now

The White House = huh? hot sweetie

White Knight = with the King

White Star = this water

Who is John Galt = jogs with Lohan…O, hangs with J. Lo

Who Wrote the Bible = two Eli, both Hebrew

Whose Line Is It Anyway = ahoy, insanely, wise wit

Who Wants to be a Millionaire = oh wow, I'm a brain on satellite…slow elimination, what a bore…to win a show, I am intolerable…oh wow, it is an abnormal elite…oh wow, I'm a total, senile brain…oh wow, I am brilliant, no tease…who am I? an illiterate snob, ow…I am wise, honorable, total win…oh wow, it's intolerable mania…abilities? a moron won wealth…I'm a late show, noble win ratio…win a lot or, I mean, I blew a host…on hit, ambition, we all answer

Wile E. Coyote and the Roadrunner = try a cartoon duel where none die

Will a Comet Hit the Earth = to hell with it, the camera!

William Shakespeare's Antony and Cleopatra = snake poisons were lethal act in a play drama

Othello by William Shakespeare = a Moor's play with a belle he likes…Moor kills a sweetie, he'll pay, bah!

Othello = hell, too

William Shakespeare's Romeo and Juliet = Oh Jesus, well, I'm a dreamlike separation…seems in-laws jeer ideal marital hook-up

Romeo and Juliet by William Shakespeare = shame I kill ideal joy between paramours…the jealous libido makes war in mere play…horrible Italian jealousy deems PM wake…play: I'll make jibe with amorous serenade

William Shakespeare's Tragic Venus and Adonis = a spurning wan love-sick maid, he dies, alas tears

The Sonnets of William Shakespeare = in fame, his talent was peerless. Oh, OK…no fearless poet like what's his name?

William Shakespeare's Birthday = April skies: we may hail the Bard

Wimbledon = me bold win

The Wimbledon Tennis Championships = bitch Henman lost, no? whipped in semi…Henman's time: he'd lob, chip, spin to win?

The Wimbledon Lawn Tennis Tournament = new balls! Tim Henman to win? end not true

Wimbledon Tennis Championship = Tim Henman win possible? do pinch!

Wimbledon Tennis Championships = I'm clownish Henman: dippiest snob…miss, do no spin/chip, Henman blew it!

The Wimbledon Championships = posh Tim Henman chips lob

wide

Windows ME = we snow'd 'im...new wisdom?

Windows Ninety-Eight = weighty, new DOS, in nit?

Winnie the Pooh = hope within one

Winnie the Pooh, Walt Disney's = went to slide his paw in honey

With All Due Respect = well-suited chapter...well hated pictures...the well-suited crap...lewd, sharp-cut elite

Within Earshot = I won't hear this

Women's Lib = blows mine...new limbos...I blow men...womb lines

Won = now...own

Word Games = we do 'grams'...we'd orgasm

Workers of the World Unite = 'work to rule,' the fine words

World Cup = crowd pul...Lord, up W.C....Dr. Low Cup

World Leaders = Orwell's dread...'r Orwell's dead

World Trade Center = lewd terror act, end...err, clattered down

The World Trade Center = the Cold War deterrent...let down the red crater...alert the tender crowd...tentacled Order threw...rattle drenched tower...rendered total wretch...wretched laden rotter

World Trade Center Attack = a crackdown, deter tattler

September Eleventh, Two Thousand and One = Oh, let's never doubt that men need weapons...detest heaven-sent hope, brutal demon now...thou sent new blood-spattered men, heaven...Oh, even torment, stop Laden, he went abused...never the debate on Laden, he must stop now...the latent war depends on Bush. even me, too...one top event, Bush's theorem: Laden wanted...new top event: Bush sent Laden to me, Oh dear...stop there, Taleban wound even the demons...O Bush never poet. Laden's men went to death...note towers' top, men. even Bush hated Laden...the penous event: both towers Laden named...the worst event! he, demon, planned to abuse...two home-bound planes threatened events

World Wide Web = bored? idle? w.w.w....lewd bride, wow!

The World Wide Web = hot, lewd, weird web

World Wrestling Federation = frown, it is not well-regarded...if odd groaners, well-written?

Worship Satan = wrath, passion

X-Rated Films = sex-mad flirt

X-Rated Movies = sex video-mart

Yale University = true Elysian Ivy...ya, sure, tiny evil...Ivy: I slay tenure...evil unity years...entirely Ivy, USA...I try uneasy evil...invite us yearly...I've yearly units...vanity us, eerily

Yankee Doodle Dandy = added an on-key yodel...dead on key? no, deadly

Yankee Stadium Urinals = make us lied, unsanitary...sulky idea man urinates...in as murkily nauseated

Year Two Thousand = a year to shut down...warns you to death...warns: death to you

The Year Two Thousand = oh, that's your date?

Yellow Submarine = O use my brain well

Yosemite Sam = seems I'm a toy

You Can't Ever Go Back Home = groovy, ace make-out bench

You Only Live Twice = yo, win lovely cutie

You've Got Mail = I'm a guy to love

Anagram Navigation

How to use the Anagramacron: If this book has inspired an interest in anagrams and the 'magic' behind them, the ideal solution is to acquire the 'Anagram Genius' software program and see for yourself. Write anything in the search-engine like you would use Google and push the button. "Perfect" anagrams rarely appear; most names of people and things do not have them. Then some strange "speaking" anagrams suddenly appear at the top of the long list of certain people and certain things. Marked "100%" sensible anagram-combinations of letters that form clear phrases and sentences are utterly fascinating and deserve close examination. These special, perfect ones are also designated in a BLUE color while anagrams less than 100% are in black.

If you do not do your own study with generators, then let the Anagramacron collection be your guide into a mysterious universe. These pages contain two years of work where everything and anything "under the sun" that came to mind was typed into 'Anagram Genius' and the results were recorded. Research has been done for you. Basically, read computer print-outs of a 'Voice' that appears to have extraordinary wisdom. Is it the Voice of Reason and Justice or something else?

My first anagram article was posted more than 10 years ago and called **"Secret World of Anagrams."** The title produced an anagram that was typical of usual first reactions upon hearing of anagram mysticism: **"arrogant defamers scowl."** Where have we been to not have heard of the phenomenon? Why is it news and not common knowledge? Was this kept from us?

To use this SMALL encyclopedia properly, do indeed check to see if the sentences, phrases and words are correct anagrams. You can quickly check in a few ways: Count the letters on one side of the 'equals.' Make sure there is the same number of letters on the other side of the 'equals.' Or pick a specific letter: if there are 3 of the letter 'a' on one side, there has to be 3 of the letter 'a' on the other and in each of the given anagrams only separated by a "…" If there are unusual letters like "q," "x," "y" or "z," they also must match precisely on the other side of the equation. Readers will observe all letters match or should match (minus a rare type-O) and absolutely no letters were intentionally added to cheat and form 'anagrams.'

Anagrams are a bit scary, because...

Anagrams are like math. It is nearly impossible to argue with math.

It's like holding a (-) mirror up to particular people and to particular things. Anagrams are a test. Will the subject anagrammed shine positively or will the subject fail us and leave us bitterly disappointed? Why not turn a microscope or telescope on a 'book' or a person and see beyond the outside exterior? Anagrams could be like a compass or Truth-Meter. Readers were asked to give "villains" the anagram-test. We know historical bad guys like "Osama," "Hitler," "Stalin" and other leaders were notorious killers and mass-murderers. What do anagrams 'say' or express about certain celebrated elites? Shouldn't we look at everything with the following meter?

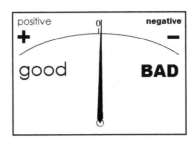

Anagrams are a means to instantly hit common, well-known beliefs and vast arrays of deep hidden truths. In most cases, it is "crazy" information we do not want to know. In most cases, it's bad news and very real. We know what bad words are and what good words are. We know the negative from the positive. See anagrams: for "Barack Obama," "George Bush," "Bill Clinton," "Houses of Parliament," "Disneyland" and their many alternate variations. Punch in official organizations of the world we live in. Give everything the 'anagram-litmus test' and see the results. Why not? It happens at the push of a button...

Possibly, the problem with new/controversial information uncovered by anagrams rests in our minds. We're products of a (brainwashed) society and Media that greatly influences us. On one hand, it's hard to understand how switched-around letters can inform us of anything. On the same hand, it's extremely difficult to believe the information itself, especially when it has darkened or tarnished some beloved, respected people and institutions.

Various groups, politicians, world leaders, actors, sports and music figures and other "stars" we thought we knew: *maybe we didn't at all?* Maybe Media has misled us, but anagrams do not.

Note numerous alternatives of names and things that also have very similar anagrams. They almost all point to the same conclusions; each seems to confirm the others. [They're usually bad].

Compare the cascade of anagrams for the "United States of America" and its variations with anagrams for "Union of Soviet Specialists Republic." When gibberish should be the results, instead: USA anagrams produced were distinctly American (Mac and fries) while Russian anagrams were specifically Russian (Stalin, Lenin, Putin).

The enigmas were endless…

If readers removed a key word within an anagrammed phrase, the rest of the words tended to be sensible and pointed to basically the same conclusions again and again. Also, the rest of the phrase/sentence remained in the identical context. Why? And in others of the same subject? Anagrams nearly force us to view the worst of horrendous secrets and vile acts as well as enlighten us toward the positive and good end of the spectrum.

Anagrams desperately expressed precise information even when they didn't have enough letters to do so, or the wrong letters. 'They' misspelled anagrams; left letters out; fudged the whole phrase because of a lack of a letter or two. Yet, the gist of the anagram was perfectly clear and intact, made sense and probably was reality. A few examples: "Taleban" for 'Taliban,' "rude" for 'ride,'etc. "F**k" and "c**ts" were used repeatedly.

Use anagrams as a tool to unravel great mysteries of the past or currently. What really happened behind the scenes of huge events such as 9/11, the Kennedy assassination and the death of Princess Diana? Or the Titanic, or the Moon landing, alien contact: old curiosities and other unknowns? Wouldn't you like to see what anagram-answers displayed that concerned big questions of our times and other times?

Lightning struck the same spot again and again and again when it came to strange anagram oddities. Each anagram and anagrams of the subjects' variations pushed us toward a similar direction or a particular viewpoint: confirmation and support of their reality. Of course, there were silly, abstract ones that sounded like cartoony Dr. Seuss things. And pure coincidences. Yet if you examine them also, there remained hints of what the prime, perfect ones revealed.

The bizarre data is so easily acquired these days with anagram-generators, shouldn't we just dive into this [ancient] new world and LISTEN to what was broadcasted?

The Mystery

Compare the anagrams of females, whether they were real people or fictional people: Were the anagrams describing feminine things, what women or girls did? Consider the anagrams of males, real or fictional: Were they describing masculine things, what guys did? Of the sensible ones with nearly perfect sentences and phrases, you'll find the 'Voice' was very accurate and pointed to the proper sex of the person anagrammed. Anagrams gauged sex and came down on the right sex when the phrases should be neutral, asexual. Why didn't masculine anagrams form from female-subjects? Why weren't feminine anagrams created by male-subjects anagrammed? Readers of this book or those familiar with 'Anagram Genius' will find that almost invariably...

Anagrams are correct sex-meters, basically. And much more.

If the person anagrammed was a known homosexual, anagrams generally informed us of this.

Anagrams often got the country of the person anagrammed right and showed the language.

The inexplicable oddity was the question: "Wait a minute. A person is male or female or a mixture of the two. But how can words (names) be masculine or feminine? They're just LETTERS!" We've assigned different sexes to various things and names. To the Anagram Voice or common sense: It is not a person or thing in the real/physical world that is anagrammed, it is a group of neutral, asexual letters. Yet, the 'speaking' anagrams got it right, over and over again.

Why do letters of infamous bad guys and bad ladies just happen to be comprised of negative, evil, mean, destructive anagrams? You'll see that they do. [Did readers view Osama's and Obama's and Bush's anagrams?] Anagrams also are Negative and Positive-meters or good and bad indicators. Wouldn't it be wonderful to know if a world leader, politician or religious leader was really a decent human being...or a homicidal maniac?

Consider the switched-letters in the name of a particular American president, for example. Why did anagrams get the Party absolutely correct? Republicans were never described as

TS Caladan

Democrats and Democrats were never described as Republicans. Again, when anagrams should only be nonsensical and be close to the mark RARELY and by sheer coincidence…

The letters mysteriously anagrammed by modern computer software *rung true* ~

With all the lies of Media, political deceptions and dark agendas from commercials, talk shows, entertainment venues and the news: maybe we urgently need to hear another voice, another view of the universe? Not saying anagrams are the Voice of God or the 100% TRUTH in everything and everyone anagrammed. I am saying anagrams are general, reliable Truth-meters. Maybe we need to hear another voice in the madness? Do anagrams show sense or rational sanity?

I'm reminded of the classic myth of Nemesis. Nemesis is the female figure our court system has *blindfolded.* You've see her statue in court. They do not want real justice and the actual truth to be known. The State, over time, has 'masked the truth.' Nemesis is not our enemy; she is our friend. She sees Evil and instantly, directly, destroys it! [Like Superman]. So says mythology. Could anagrams do the same, in the sense of immediately piercing bullshit and striking at the heart of Truth?

Ten years ago, when it dawned on me that perfect/jumbled letters SPOKE, I listened and recorded. Strangely, I 'scratched my head' about many celebrities and other famous people when I viewed their anagrams. Why was nearly everyone so dark and negative? People, historically, highly regarded skilled performers or writers or actors or musicians…

Did almost all of them have 'skeletons in closets' and horrible hidden secrets? I was befuddled.

Today it is a very different story. Thank you YouTube. Today we can search through the lies and bullshit and *sometimes* arrive at revelations and marvelous truths discovered by courageous investigators. 'Everything' is there for us to discover, if we only took the time and looked and put the pieces together with open eyes. Ah, ha! What a difference in the last 10 years, from what I once believed in total ignorance/misguidance and what I've discovered recently:

Back then, I knew Church and State were bad news: *just God-*

awful. I did not understand that even our heroes and celebrities they insisted are and were "great," really weren't that great. *What, the Beatles weren't that good? Oh, my God.*

This applies to anagrams in the sense: Was the 'Voice of Anagrams' a mean demon from the evil, occult side 'painting good things black' and being a nasty bugger, voice of the Devil? OR. Were we 'hearing' and seeing pure TRUTH, displayed in English letters over and over again?

Ten years later, this author of conspiracies would testify: "Oh, this was real and hardly ever revealed earlier. It's an uncomfortable, inconvenient exposure we don't really enjoy hearing and seeing."

Who knows? People fear the unknown, and the ancient technique of anagramming is a major mystery. Anagrams might not be a devilish fortune-teller machine we've seen in a 'Twilight Zone' deli or a portal to a Ouija dimension of Black Magic, one that is a con, a lure, a lie and a negative trap for mankind. What IF (and it's a big if) anagrams were the voices of good, positive Angels of Justice that essentially shined enlightenment upon us? *Somewhat.*

Why aren't anagrams popular or widely known for their weird mysticism and uncanny accuracy as well as fated prognostication? (Many elites were born with the names that held their later destiny).

The answer might be for the same reason Nemesis was blindfolded or why true history was changed by those in power to favor those in power. It's why truth was hidden by extremely powerful Secret Societies that rule the world. They are not going to let you know of your true history and true divinity. They don't reveal truth or give away power. Instead, they've made us 'warlike animals' when nothing was and is further from reality. No big publishing house of London or New York will ever promote an Anagram Encyclopedia like the **Anagramacron**. *Or Oprah.* (Thank You, TWB Press) To turn a Media spotlight on atrocities and terrible crimes alive on Earth, presently and in the past, to call attention, bring to the surface long-buried, occulted realities. Ouija Boards take all day. What's in crystal balls? Real psychics are expensive. Anagram generators are available and large archives of

'The Voice of Anagrams' digitally lay there, online. Were anagrams informing us of the harsh truths of the real world?

Dark, inconceivable facts also remain tucked away in libraries, old books and even on some YouTube. Who takes time to study? Most of us are lazy and confidently believe the information of Media, the feds, schools and universities, rather than take the time to QUESTION all things we're told and honestly investigate on our own. We send our children to (training, indoctrination) schools, rather than 'Getting Smart' ourselves and homeschooling the children we love.

Most of all, wherever correctness lay and whatever we're dealing with, **we need open minds**.

A Little Anagram History

According to some historians, anagrams originated in the 4th Century B.C. with the Greek poet Lychophon. He used them to impress the rich and famous. Other sources suggest that in the 6th Century B.C., Pythagoras used anagrams to discover Life's philosophical meanings and great truths. Plato and his followers believed that anagrams revealed divinity and one's personal "destiny." In early Roman times, anagrams were thought to have mystical or prophetic powers. Jewish Cabalists in the 13th Century were aware of *anagram mysticism* and their significance. Secret Societies, down through the ages, enjoyed the occult messages hidden within anagrams. In the 16th and 17th Centuries, some controversial scientists such as Galileo recorded their theories in anagram form. The French King, Louis XIII, appointed Thomas Billon as his Royal Anagramist.

Nostradamus predicted Napoleon's rise to power in France and wrote his name: "Pau Nay Loron" in basically an anagram. The letters rearranged result in "Napaulon Roy" or Napoleon.

Today, switched-around letters are considered amusing word games and brainteasers. We have lost what could be the actual (very complex) significance of anagrams. Were the ancients far more aware of the deeper meanings in Life? Did they know the secret relevance of anagrams and much more? Are we only beginning to understand what's been lost over the centuries?

From the Encyclopedia Americana:

"Anagrams date from ancient times. Composing them was a favorite pastime during the Middle Ages, when a mystic connection was believed to exist between the nature or fate of a person and an anagram derived from his name."

"(Anagrams are)…as significant as the Bible Code, Da Vinci Code, the Kabala, numerology and many other mystic arts that contain embedded information, indicating a web work of other-dimensional connections between seemingly unrelated things."

- Leo Scarpelli

TS Caladan

"Mystics and new-agers will tell you that anagrams can offer a glimpse into the soul or essence of that thing or person."

- Internet

Paul Hunt is a respected researcher into UFOs and other metaphysical subjects and former owner of the 'Atlantis Bookstore' in Burbank, California. He was kind enough to write the following words for my proposed manuscript called 'The Anagram Code' ten years ago:

"Anagrams are interesting and entertaining ways to exercise the mind. They have also been used to conceal messages, a game that became an important method of sending coded messages. But the basic roots of the anagram, in the lost dim past of mankind's development of language, present us with evidence that there is possibly a divine or spiritual significance to it all. We have at the very dawn of the Christian era, a famous Latin anagram, an answer formed from a question that Pontius Pilate asked: *"Quid est veritas?"* [What is truth?] The answer, *"Est vir qui adest"* [It is the man who is here]. This may well be the greatest anagram and the most important to the western world. Then we have a word that is close to an anagram: anagoge. It pertains to literature and seeks to extract a spiritual message from language, that there is a secret or occult message that references things of spiritual significance. Is it possible that in our language the very words themselves have covert meanings? Doug Yurchey (TS Caladan) has spent a great deal of effort in researching this question. He presents an incredible selection of hidden meanings within names, things, places, fictional titles, events and politics. Could this all be coincidence? He has indeed given us some serious 'food for thought' and explores the mind-twisting and astonishing truths behind anagrams. Be warned: **This is absolutely literary intoxication and addiction!**"

What happens if all 26 letters of the alphabet were placed in an anagram-generator? The following phrases are known as "pangrams."

Mr. Jock, TV quiz PhD, bags few lynx

Meg Schwarzkopf quit Jynx Blvd.
Fox-TV clad QPR gems whiz by junk
foxy, waltzing, dumb, PVC HQ jerks
block VD HQ mix frenzy, just gawp
fix TV knob, lewd GHQ jumps crazy
KGB wants quiz PhD Lexy from JVC
blowzy night frumps vex'd Jack Q

'ANAGRAMMATISM' is a real word and describes a long lost art.
An`a`gram´ma`tism   n. 1. The act or practice of making anagrams

Special thanks must be given to Howard W. Bergerson and his book 'Palindromes and Anagrams.' The book was published in 1973 and contains more than 1100 anagrams. The surprise is many of those found by the author have relevance to the subject anagrammed. In other words, he found numerous examples of 'IT' or the strange, informed 'Voice' decades before the age of computer search-engines. Mr. Bergerson should be applauded as a modern pioneer in the "Secret World of Anagrams."

In the July 31st ('06) issue of Sports Illustrated, a sportswriter wrote: "Anagrams, when used correctly, cut through the BS." He wrote of Sports in an article that showed some anagrams of modern athletes. Yet, researchers of Anagram Mysticism discovered that weird letter-transpositions occurred in a myriad of subjects. *Possibly every subject.* He was correct in the assessment that anagrams cut to the heart of the matter and seemed to be very smart. If you can't trust a sportswriter, who *can* you trust?

More Anagram Mysticism

"I did not make a discovery of coincidence." ~ Doug Yurchey
"Don't mistake coincidence for fate." ~ Mr. Eko

What's in anagrams? Could be answers to Life, the Universe and Everything!

Skeptics and cynics explained the world with the realistic 'sword' of 'Occam's Razor.' The concept was that the *simplest* ideas were the most real. Razor? Was the term meant to cut through the BS and arrive at the simple, plain truth. Who said the great Secrets of the Universe, the Big/Philosophical Questions in Life, were simple? Only the simple-minded would think so. Don't be narrow. We have to expect the unexpected. That's the pattern. It's what independent researchers will discover, time and time again. Incredible things are the nature of the real world. We have to be complex-minded, future-minded. We have to sincerely wonder about our fantastic and extremely serendipitous universe. We have to ask important questions. Do not fear the pursuits of answers to those questions. Do not fear what we'll learn ~

The lesson or bottom line is you can understand more truth by being positive rather than being negative. Absolutely stay OPEN. Do not conclude before you have done an investigation. But do an investigation. It is not 'every wild idea is true.' However, the truth, the reality under the surface, is usually unbelievable, inconceivable and very far-out!

Like quatrains of Michel de Nostradamus, anagrams were matters of interpretation, a type of poetry or literature as prophetic and profound destiny. It's not a new concept. Study anagrams beyond the extent of this small encyclopedia. Find out for yourself and be your own teacher. Reexamine controversial anagrams. Learn. They contain another side, another view, drastically divergent from bogus information forced upon us by Media and other sources in today's society.

They lie. Those few in control, at the top of the social pyramid, lie to us human beings on the lower levels. They lie to us constantly, so much so: It's like there's no deception at all.

Possibly, everything is in plain sight. Maybe we only need the key to unlock 'oceans' of secrets?

Something bizarre and insightful **SPEAKS** to us in the form of the perfect anagrams. Something tries very hard to reach us from great depths, or is IT from light-years away? Or another world? Even if IT does not have the right letters, IT still persists in the broadcast of strange and consistent knowledge, again and again. I insist...

We should simply LISTEN. We have the mature ability to feel or decipher the truth for ourselves. We have the right to get it wrong, but also the right to get it right. We can discard the silliness and absurdities in transposed letters. We can be moved by the information or 'Voice' of anagrams. We can also learn and grow and change because of them.

Refer to the Anagramacron. Spread the information around like 'secrets of an occult (hidden) underground.' 'Waters' that readers should really test are those of 'Anagram Genius.' The software is worth the price. Have super journeys. I can only hope your fascination-level reaches mine.

We conclude with a mystery that sure would interest the Sherlock Holmes character. What if anagrams revealed the identity of the infamous, murderous, Jack the Ripper?

Richard Wallace, author of **'Jack the Ripper, Light-Hearted Friend'** (Gemini Press, 1996), spent 25 years in the data processing field. His book revealed that Lewis Carroll loved anagrams. He believed anagrams held deep truths. It has been discovered that many lines in Carroll's poetry and stories form perfect anagrams. Some people believe that 19th Century author of 'Alice in Wonderland' confessed to being the Ripper in numerous, perfect anagrams: The following quote was also spoken verbatim by Johnny Depp I Tim Burton's file 'Alice Through the Looking Glass':

'Twas brillig, and the slithy toves, Did gyre and gimble in the wabe: All mimsy were the borogoves. And the mome raths outgrabe = I bet I beat my glands til, with hand-sword I slay the evil gender, slimey theme, borrow gloves, bag, and masturbate the hog more...he, Lewis, grabbed the vibrant role, assembled dreams and rhymes with glee, but vowed that one most mighty goal: originality. [This famous line by Carroll is composed of exactly 100 letters].

Richard Wallace's book was excerpted in the November 1996 Harper's. Jacobson and Heaney wrote: "The first paragraph of [Wallace's] article contains a grisly confession."

This is my story of Jack the Ripper, the man behind Britain's worst unsolved murders. It is a story that points to the unlikeliest of suspects: a man who wrote children's stories. That man is Charles Dodgson, better known as Lewis Carroll, author of such beloved books as Alice in Wonderland = the truth is this: I, Richard Wallace, stabbed and killed a muted Nicole Brown in cold blood, severing her throat with my trusty shiv's strokes. I set up Orenthal James Simpson, who is utterly innocent of this murder. PS: I also wrote Shakespeare's sonnets and a lot of Francis Bacon's works too.

Were words that concerned a description of the O.J. "murder" simply in the air in the middle of the 1990s? Did anagrams bring them to the surface, recorded in Wallace's book? What connection was there to Shakespeare and Francis Bacon? Was there one? Were anagrams informing us that the similarity was in the fact of a grand deception and public lies?

Wallace's book has come under heavy criticism, as you might have imagined. The following anagrams are perfect anagrams that have resulted from the transposition of letters directly taken from Carroll's 19th Century poetry. We have Wallace to thank. But the quotes came from a harsh skeptic of anagrams and a dreadful critic of the speculation in Wallace's book. Possibly…

Insiders of power and prestige and Media manipulation know the royal secret of "the Ripper" while the general public remains clueless. We have been fed generations of 'Alice in Wonderland' stories like we are fed generations of Disney productions and Hollywood Magic. 'They've' made us believe: There are no evil agendas and dark motives behind the colorful Oz fantasies we've given our children as entertainment. Maybe anagrams inform us of something different. You decide if the next anagrams or quotes have finally told us the horrible truth. Why have so many sources ridiculed and blasted Wallace's book? Were they 'protesting too much' when they repeatedly insisted the idea was absurd and anagrams were nothing more than coincidences?

"Then d'file noses, lad."

"Rip no gay peter foreskin."

"Felt kid yen."

"I slit nine throats."

"Seed a mother, don."

"Beg, dole, evil whores, I tax all tits."

"Defend the loin, lass."

"A raw hymen felt rough, horrid."

"Sin thee, fondle lads."

"Ah, pants and orgasm, hero-poet I am."

"Moan, true bitch."

"He kept the jar of uteri enclosed in vase."

"Few fellow dons give phony love to man's mouth, wet arse."

I have to remind readers that anagrams should express the nonsensical and the abstract, not relate and reveal intimacies of the subjects anagrammed. These old anagrams, before computers, once more, indicate extremely vile acts upon the youth of both sexes. Possibly, through movies and television, we have been force-fed 'Jack the Ripper' MYTHS, on purpose, so we don't know the truth? He was a doctor. He hated prostitutes. He was Royalty. Maybe he was only a bloody/sick madman named Charles Dodgson (Carroll), sponsored by Royalty and by the highest halls of deception and lies?

The critic here, who blasted Wallace yet provided the quotes, claimed COINCIDENCE in every, single example, without seeing the corroboration in anagrams or examining the information itself. To the (paid) critic: All was nonsense. Anagrams were nonsense. Like a person who argued against the possibility of Life in the universe, they're ignorant mind was made up, first, or they pushed very forcefully an agenda against rational thoughts and reasoning.

No one should demand how we are to think. Fascists would. You decide for yourself. Scan as much of the evidence as you can, openly. When you see someone blindly, unscientifically, who pushed an agenda HARD…question the motives of that person. The critic played upon everyone not being educated on what anagrams actually were, their history, and what priceless gems they contained. What would the guy think of the Anagramacron collection?

The critic ripped to shreds the following quotes and the whole concept. Let's criticize the critic who might be paid-off by elites who understood very well the Power of Anagrams. Let's consider the next info from Wallace's 1996 book 'Jack the Ripper, Light-Hearted Friend,' only not under sharp cynicism or absurdity, but under the fair and just scrutiny of Eyes Wide Open…

"Dodgson, disguised as a clerk, bought a knife, took trains, stayed in his London house. He'd help the fates. How? A hump from behind, cut a whore in the face, masturbate. Wash up."

"Let not holier thoughts reveal cheap animal mores."

"No one shall spanketh the hot male meat, and the hot male meat shall spanketh no one."

"They, the Uranian kings, often hit on night fags."

"Is it coincidence?" Wallace asked, "…that one of the victims was found barely a block from Collingwood Street?" 'Collingwood' was Dodgson's sister Mary's married name. [One of the White Chapel victims was named "Alice"].

Lewis Carroll quoted from Hamlet in 'Sylvie and Bruno' and Harry Furniss illustrated 'Sylvie and Bruno.' The illustrator's name was mentioned in one of the anagrams:
The funeral-baked meats did coldly furnish forth the marriage tables = Harry Furniss called me a harsh, demented tart, but I faked the glib fool

Another piece of evidence Wallace alluded to was that the Ripper might not have worked alone. Were the Ripper killings done by an organized (Jesuit) Hit Squad, financed by Parliament to cause chaos? The critic slammed Wallace's connection with an "elite" chap known as Thomas Vere Bayne, a dean at Oxford. Yet, history records that Vere Bayne and Lewis Carroll did indeed know of the other. Were they more than friends? Were they partners in terrible crimes?

He thought he saw an Albatross that fluttered round the lamp: He looked again and found it was a Penny-Postage Stamp. "You'd best be getting home," he said. "The nights are very damp." = Thomas Vere Bayne penned, posted a 'Dear Boss' letter to the papers in red ink. He'd laugh with a fit at the thought of getting hounds to bag us. We dandy, gay sons: a hump, hate all, Mama!

Lewis Carroll wrote in his diary every day in purple ink. But on the night Ripper victim Catherine Eddowes was murdered, he wrote his entry in **black** ink. The next day, Carroll was back to purple ink. Did this happen on other occasions?

From *The Hunting of the Snark:*

"They sought it with thimbles, they sought it with care:

They pursued it with forks and with hope;

They threatened its life with a railway share;

They charmed it with smiles and soap."

We know from various police reports that the dead women had a "thimble," a "fork" and "soap" (among other things) in their pockets at the time of their deaths.

Dodgson's short stories also contained the same violent, "masturbatory" and perverted themes. IF Dodgson was the true author of all the complex anagrams and huge volumes of stories [he might not have been], how did he do it? Could it have been in the same vein that Shakespeare was not the true author of his masterworks? (Or the Beatles?) Maybe it was done and sanctioned and financed by royal committee. *Even the murders~*

In 'The Walking Stick of Destiny,' he created two characters' names from anagrams. "Baron Slogdod" translated to "Dodgson Labor" and "Signor Blowski" meant: "I blow gross kin."

Wallace found a letter that Charles Dodgson (Lewis Carroll) wrote to his sister, Lizzy. It contained two anagrams according to Wallace and according to our eyes:

I believe in the Doctrine of Eternal Punishment = I'd be proven insane if I let the lion meet her cunt...I believe the Fathers condemn penile nutrition

The critic condemned Wallace for his belief in anagrams as

amazing indicators. He blasted the author when he noticed that the anagrams, again and again, showed the same sick perversions. The critic was not in awe, as any reasonable person should have been. Similar anagrams do not nullify the great mystery, they intensified it! I've described the phenomenon as "Lightning bolts striking the same spot over and over."

Wallace's conclusions were taken from hundreds of examples in Carroll's poetry and other writings. A large number were cited in his book. Wasn't it peculiar that Dodgson's anagrams, anagrams of savagery and awful violence against the young, repeated the same sick themes over and over? What if truth were so far removed from reality? The critic blamed the author for outrageous claims in his book: Yet, in every example, Richard Wallace proved his point. The anagrams absolutely portrayed common themes of sexual imagery, anal intercourse, erotic violence, murder and death of women and children. Why? Have elites of the world, through the generations, told us again and again of real atrocities hidden in children's stories?

The following was the critic's final conclusions. Please feel free to agree or disagree. But if the Anagramacron has showed you anything at all, it's showed readers that anagrams are *not* silly word-games. They are great unknowns. They are something far, far more than we believe ~

"Anagrams, in fact, aren't significant. Especially not in a positional language like English. They are funny coincidences at best, like the fact that "Clint Eastwood" is an anagram for "Old West Action." Literary kooks go for anagrams because they can always find exactly what they're after. Take, for example, all the anagrams purporting to prove that Francis Bacon did (or didn't) write the works attributed to Shakespeare. I wouldn't really recommend this book to anyone -- it's desperately badly written, to the point of being nearly unreadable, and poorly organized. What you find in it will leave you pinching the bridge of your nose and shaking your head so often that your friends will ask if you have a sinus headache. There is a great deal more nuttiness in the book than I've chosen to highlight in this review. I think this book is another example of the Kennedy Conspiracy Delusion. It's intolerable to some people that major events could have been brought about by chance, or that a notorious crime could have been committed by an obscure loser. *Jack the Ripper: "Light-Hearted Friend"* is a dramatic demonstration that some people shouldn't be allowed near a Scrabble set. As an example of literary scholarship gone horribly wrong…"

At the very least, the perfect anagrams are fairly accurate meters of good and bad, indicators of positive and negative and can distinguish heroes from villains and wolves in 'sheep's clothing.' Maybe we should utilize the computer software program of **'Anagram Genius'** to find more fascinating treasures and mysteries to uncover in the past, present and future.

ANAGRAMACRON

Tray Samuel Caladan = actually sane drama … a natural, aces madly … dearly as actual man … a smart-alec? nay: dual … a man reads, actually … arty, casual lad, amen … as actually n a dream … neat dream, casually … am as a nerd, actually … a real casualty, damn … lays an actual dream … ace art, sad manually … am actually near sad … am sadly an ultra ace … lay a mature scandal … ultra as a May candle … stale Macaulay, darn … a calm, unready Atlas … man, Atlas, ultra decay … am a lunacy star deal … and a small, acute Ray … and may actual laser … my lad as an ace ultra … actual salary named … actual salary amend … an adult salary came … rascal and a tale, yum … sad man era, actually … sadly came a natural … as natural lady came … am easy carnal adult … casual dream, neatly … randy as actual male … as a duly carnal mate … manual acts lay dear … a saucy, maternal lad … a damn saucy lateral … as damn ace ultra lay … lay a mad cruel Satan … duly alarm ace Satan … a malady, ulcer Satan … tea and casually ram … saner mad, actually … manual acts already … casually made an art … casual arty and meal … manly ace, a duel star … a lunacy dream Atlas … manually at a sacred … casual tale and army … casual male and arty … mate casually ran, da … lay amateur scandal … an alarmed casualty … am sad ace, naturally … and casual May alert … a sadly clean trauma … an am casually rated … as actual, manly read … an at dream, casually … manually cased a rat … casually made a rant … cruel data, manly as a … mad, actual analyser … as dear cat manually … casually trade an arm … as a clean, adult arm … cleanly, a sad trauma … and actual alarm, yes … a tar and me, casually … my natural as ace lad … lane casualty drama … a manual car sly date ... a me and art, casually ... actually mad arenas ... an actual ram delays ... cat manuals already ... a cat reads manually ... a Tray and a small cue ... casually a named art ... casual at nearly mad ... man as dare, actually ... an ultra cam, analysed ... an adult camera lays ... delay a natural scam ... a smart/clean dual, ya ... an amateurs' call day ... alarm as a nudely cat ... lunacy as a male, drat ... a damn actual slayer ... rate mad lunacy, alas ... my Dracula Satan ale ... Dracula Satany meal ... am as a clean duly rat ... am a cruel lady Satan ... (Well, you can't believe all anagrams).

TS Caladan = at scandal

Douglas Stephen Yurchey = young-eyed, chapters lush ... angels' cushy, deputy hero ... honestly aches, super-guy ... huge honesty, up sacredly ... the only crude, pushy sage ... hyped guru, honestly aces ... launch speedy, gutsy hero

Enjoy more writing from TS Caladan

 The Continuum (TWB Press, 2014)
A sci-fi novel by Tray Caladan
http://www.twbpress.com/thecontinuum.html

 Son of Zog (TWB Press, 2015)
A sci-fi novel by Tray Caladan
http://www.twbpress.com/sonofzog.html

 The Cydonian War (TWB Press, 2016)
A sci-fi novel by TS Caladan
http://www.twbpress.com/thecydonianwar.html

Science-Faction (TWB Press, 2017)
An alternate sci-fi anthology by TS Caladan
http://www.twbpress.com/sciencefaction.html

TS Caladan

http://www.twbpress.com

Science Fiction – Supernatural – Horror - Thriller

www.ingramcontent.com/pod-product-compliance
Lightning Source LLC
Chambersburg PA
CBHW071115050326
40690CB00008B/1228

* 9 7 8 1 9 4 4 0 4 5 3 4 0 *